THE FLIGHT ATTENDANT CAREER GUIDE

Tim Kirkwood

Written and compiled by Tim Kirkwood
Edited by Jeanne Gibbons Plummer
Book design by Rick Barry

Published by TKE Publishing
P.O.Box 6455
Delray Beach, FL 33484-6455
Printed in the USA

Kirkwood, Timothy L.
    The flight attendant career guide / Timothy L. Kirkwood.
    p. cm.
    Presigned LCCN: 93-85322
    ISBN 0-9637301-4-2

    1. Flight attendants--Vocational guidance. I. Title.

HD8039.A43K57 1993   387.7'4044'023
                                         QBI93-1269

Library of Congress Catalog Card Number: 93-85322

Cover Printed on Recycled Paper

✈ TABLE OF CONTENTS

Introduction   1

History of Flight Attendants   3

Flight Attendant Unions   9

Minimum Requirements for the Job   10

Education is the Key   11

Let's Get Physical   13

Work Experience That Counts   15

Attitude, Attitude, Attitude   17

Career Benefits   19

Types of Airlines   21

The Application Process   23

How to Shine in the Interview   27

Congratulations, You're Hired!   31

Flight Scheduling   37

A Typical Three Day Trip   41

Your Future in the Skies   45

Vocabulary   47

Common Airport/City Codes   53

The Airline Listings   57

Information Updates   84

 DEDICATION

This book is dedicated to those in the industry who fought long and hard to put the "pro" in professional.

✈ ACKNOWLEDGEMENTS

I would like to thank the people without whom this book would not have been possible. Special thanks to the In-Flight and Human Resources departments of the airlines for their invaluable assistance, and to the flight attendants who contributed their ideas and views. My thanks to Margaret, Vicki, Kathleen and Aysun. I am grateful to Jeanne for her tireless editing and support, and to Darlene for putting up with my many hours in front of the computer screen.   —TK

✈ ABOUT THIS GUIDE

The *FLIGHT ATTENDANT CAREER GUIDE* is intended to be a valuable escort through the complex and demanding process of obtaining the position of flight attendant with the airline of your choice. By using this guide, you will be able to concentrate on the airlines that fulfill the requirements or preferences that *you* have for your career. For the airline, it helps bring to the interviewing process candidates for employment who are knowledgeable and well-prepared for the position.

The information contained within this guide, which has been gathered from flight attendants and human resource and in-flight services departments of the listed airlines, is believed to be correct and up-to-date. Information may change without notice due to contractual changes in the industry. This guide is intended for information gathering only, and is not a guarantee of employment.

✈ INTRODUCTION

You've seen them in the movies: flying to exotic and faraway places, spending luxurious days in Paris or Rome, indulging the every whim of their wealthy (and single!) first class passengers before returning to their smartly furnished apartments in Midtown Manhattan. The passengers on their flights are all happy, sophisticated and calm, and they always have plenty of time to spend with each and every one. The airplanes they fly on are spacious and comfortable, with aisles so wide you could drive a truck down them. And they all look like models from the pages of Vogue and GQ. How could you *not* want to be a flight attendant?

Real life is much different than the movies, and you need to be fully prepared to accept this fact before you even consider the position of flight attendant. While the above scenario may have been somewhat true in the early days, deregulation of the airlines has changed the industry. Prior to deregulation, airline fares and routes were set by the U.S. Government, which made the system fair for all airlines, regardless of size. Then in 1978, those regulations were removed, and airlines were free to set fares and routes at whatever the market would bear. Survival of the fittest is now the controlling economic reality in the industry. Dollars and cents control most management decision making, and airlines must cut costs where they can. Attempting to maximize productive crew utilization has become the standard in the airline industry. This translates into more work and longer hours for the same, or lower wages. In the pages that follow, an attempt will be made to describe the "real world" of the airline flight attendant – considered by many to be the best job in the world!

✈ HISTORY OF FLIGHT ATTENDANTS

The first flight attendants were called "couriers," and they were the young sons of the steamship, railroad, and industrial magnates who financed the airlines. They served in the 1920's until the stock market crash of 1929, when their positions were eliminated to reduce operating expenses. Western Air Express was the first to employ stewards, who served on the "Model Airway" – a Los Angeles to San Francisco run, using Fokker F-10 aircraft.

During the early 1930's, the First Officers on flights would serve as cabin attendants, as well as assisting in flying the plane. But this splitting of duties proved inefficient, and airlines began to consider other options.

United was the first airline to hire women, beginning with Ellen Church in 1939. Airline executives believed that the presence of a female attendant on board would reassure passengers of the increasing safety of air travel. It would be difficult for potential travelers to admit fears of flying when young women routinely took to the air as part of the inflight crew. Further, it was believed that women would cater to the predominantly male passengers. (Not everyone was enthusiastic about the idea, though. Pilots claimed they were too busy flying to look after helpless female crew members.)

Flying on Ford Tri-motors, "stewardesses" would serve their eleven to eighteen passengers a cold picnic meal, usually consisting of fried chicken, which they had assembled prior to passenger boarding. Coffee was served out of thermos bottles. In addition to the meal service, stewardesses were also responsible for winding the clocks and altimeters in the cabin, and ensuring that the wicker passenger seats were securely bolted to the aircraft floor.

In addition to the meal service, stewardesses were also responsible for winding the clocks and altimeters in the cabin, and ensuring that the wicker passenger seats were securely bolted to the aircraft floor

They were also required to advise passengers not to throw lighted cigars and cigarettes out the aircraft windows while over populated areas, and to ensure that passengers didn't use the exit door instead of the lavatory door! All this for the exciting salary of one hundred to one hundred and fifty dollars per month.

In the beginning, the airlines preferred to only hire registered nurses, not just for their medical experience, but also because it was believed that nurses led a disciplined life which would transfer well to the rigors of airline travel. During World War II, the position of Purser was created for men only, as women were not allowed to work on the Civil Reserve Air Fleet (CRAF) flights.

The stewardess career went through many transformations over the years. The job changed from something one only did for a few years prior to marriage, to a long term career worth retaining until retirement. This has largely been a result of better wage and benefits packages secured by unions on behalf of various flight attendant work forces. In times past, stewardesses were required to quit when they married or became pregnant. Airlines hired only young women, and forced them to retire when they reached the ripe old age of 30! During the 1960's and 1970's, through the Civil Rights Act of 1964, the

Equal Opportunity Amendment, and various lawsuits, these barriers gradually fell. Now airlines must hire people of all races, ages, marital status, and gender. As more men entered the workforce, the job title was changed from "stewardess" to the current "flight attendant" or "cabin attendant".

The 1980's brought deregulation of the airline industry, and opened the way for corporate greed. Salaries were pushed back to 1970 levels, bargaining power was weakened, and over fifty-percent of the airlines which existed in pre-deregulation times went bankrupt or were forced out of business. The 90's outlook is uncertain, as more airlines are filing for protection under Chapter 11 of the bankruptcy code, even as this guide is printed. For persons considering the position of flight attendant as a long term career, it is of the utmost necessity that you *study the listings in this guide to make the most informed choice possible when selecting a carrier.* Then research the history of the airline you're considering. Possible sources of information are business newspapers and magazines. One of your best and most accessible sources might be the flight attendants who work for your preferred airline. Spend a day out at your local airport, interviewing flight attendants while they're waiting for their flights. Ask them about working conditions, rates of pay, management attitude, job security, etc. Show them your copy of

In times past, stewardesses were required to quit when they married or became pregnant.

Airlines hired only young women, and forced them to retire when they reached the ripe old age of 30!

THE FLIGHT ATTENDANT CAREER GUIDE, and ask them any questions you might have about their airline's listing. (You'll soon discover many flight attendants have used this guide while they were job hunting!)

✈ FLIGHT ATTENDANT UNIONS

The first flight attendant union was the Association of Air Line Stewardesses (AALS), formed by flight attendants of United Airlines in 1945 to combat inequality in the workplace. There are now six flight attendant unions. They are: the International Brotherhood of Teamsters (IBT), the Independent Federation of Flight Attendants (IFFA), International Association of Machinists and Aerospace Workers (IAM), Association of Flight Attendants (AFA), Association of Professional Flight Attendants (APFA), and the Transport Workers Union (TWU). If there is a union representing the employees of the carrier you wish to work for, you will be required to join the union immediately after you are hired, in order to maintain employment. There are a few airlines where flight attendants do not have the benefit of a union.

Flight attendant unions have been instrumental in securing fairness in labor contracts for their members, including good wage and benefits packages, health and life insurance, pension plans, and safe working conditions. At the same time, they have battled against sex, age and race discrimination, wrongful discipline and/or discharge, and unfair labor practices. For an excellent account of the formation of the first flight attendant union, I highly recommend picking up a copy of *"From Sky Girl To Flight Attendant"* by Georgia Panter Nielsen (ILR Press).

> Flight attendant unions have been instrumental in securing fairness in labor contracts for their members

✈ MINIMUM REQUIREMENTS FOR THE JOB

Airlines usually say they are looking for people who have pleasant personalities and who work well with people. While this is generally true, there are additional factors which can assist you in getting the job. Here are the minimums:

- U.S. citizenship, or alien registration (green card) with a work permit
- Social security card
- Excellent English skills

Passports are not required by all airlines, but applying for one now will ensure that you are prepared if it's needed.

✈ EDUCATION

A high school diploma or a G.E.D. is required for employment by *all* airlines. If you're in school now, *stay in school!* If you've dropped out, go back and get your diploma or G.E.D. No matter if you speak five languages, you will get nowhere with the airlines without a high school diploma. Most companies also prefer two years of college, primarily for the maturity this gives you. A college education will also improve your chances of securing the job, as it shows a desire to improve yourself. Courses which rate highly with the airlines are sociology, psychology, history, geography, and foreign languages. List any courses you've taken which might be applicable. Some schools even offer courses in how to be a flight attendant. And, while you're at it, take a course in first aid or cardiopulmonary resuscitation (CPR), which is offered in most cities by the American Red Cross.

While only Northwest and Executive Airlines require you to speak a foreign language in order to be hired, the more languages in which you are fluent, the better your chances of securing the job. Airlines also give preference to language of destination qualified persons when assigning flight schedules. A French-speaking flight attendant may receive priority to work Paris flights over a more senior, non-

French-speaking flight attendant, and will usually receive additional pay for those flights. You will be tested on your language ability, so list only the languages in which you are fluent – not the ones you've only begun to study.

There are many airline "schools" which advertise that they will train you and place you with an airline. For this, they will charge you a large fee or "tuition". The simple fact is: every airline will send you through their own training course, whether you've taken one of the courses these schools offer, or whether you've come from another airline, with twenty years experience as a flight attendant. Everyone starts off equally. Prior flight attendant experience or training will not exempt you from training with your next airline. Any school which charges high tuition, or promises placement with an airline should be well investigated before investing. Stick to the inexpensive adult education or community college courses.

✈ LET'S GET PHYSICAL

All airlines will give you a physical before you complete training, and *all* will give you a drug test, as required by the Department of Transportation (DOT). During your working career you will be randomly drug tested as well. If you are currently using illegal drugs, even on a sporadic or "recreational" basis, quit them at once! You will not be hired if you cannot pass a drug test. You must be in good health with all your faculties functioning. Some health conditions which may disqualify you are: high blood pressure, heart problems, chronic sinus, back, or hearing problems, and certain genetic and acquired syndromes. Your eyesight must be 20/20, or correctible to 20/20 with glasses or contacts.

Age minimum is eighteen, but may be higher with some airlines. All airlines are prohibited by law from discriminating by age, and many have realized the benefits of hiring mature individuals. It's not uncommon for a nineteen year old trainee to be seated next to a forty or fifty year old trainee in the same class. People of all ages have the desire to travel the world as part of an airline crew.

Height requirements are generally between 5' and 6', and are set to ensure that you are tall enough to reach emergency equipment and overhead compartments, and short enough to fit into the smaller aircraft. Your weight must be *in proportion to your height*. You should be in good

You should be in good physical condition as the work and the hours can be physically draining.

physical condition, as the work and the hours can be physically draining. A typical meal service on a 727 aircraft can translate into one hundred to two hundred trips walking up and down the aisles carrying food trays, possibly in the space of an hour and a half. You must be physically able to open the aircraft doors which can be quite heavy. You may also be called upon to carry passengers out of a burning aircraft or to pull them out of their seats in order to perform cardiopulmonary resuscitation.

Airlines prefer pleasant looking applicants, but not necessarily the model type. Clear complexion, absence of obvious facial scars, and neat, well-manicured hands are a must. Hair must be clean and styled; shoulder length for women and collar length for men. Longer hair is acceptable on women if it is tied back or worn up, to meet sanitary requirements for handling food. Long hair is not acceptable for men. Beards may be allowed, depending on the grooming regulations of each airline. Compliance with the airlines' published grooming regulations is mandatory. Refusal to comply with published grooming regulations may lead to discipline and/or dismissal.

✈ WORK EXPERIENCE THAT COUNTS

The best work experience you can bring to the airlines is public contact work. Dealing with the public takes practice, and you'll need all the practice you can get before dealing with hundreds of people, who are sealed in a tube which is hurtling through space at five hundred miles per hour! A prior job at Burger King means more to the airlines than a job as a Certified Public Accountant.

Sales experience is also recommended. List any public contact experience you may have had when you apply, no matter how trivial, and strive to gain additional experience prior to your interview. Any volunteer work you've done is also good, as it shows initiative on your part. If you've won any awards or recognition at your job or in your community, you'll also want to bring this to the attention of the airlines. Other good work experience is in hotels, restaurants, retail sales, travel agencies, tour guiding, customer service, car rentals, convention host/essing, airport greeting, and hospital work.

A prior job at Burger King means more to the airlines than a job as a Certified Public Accountant

✈ ATTITUDE, ATTITUDE, ATTITUDE

The most important things you will need for the flight attendant job are flexibility and a positive attitude. Flexibility is one of the requirements of the job which most flight attendants love, and it is the attribute you'll need most to succeed in the job. If it is important for you to be home every night to be with your family or to watch Wheel of Fortune, then this job is not for you. Being a flight attendant is not only a job; it's a lifestyle. It is possible you will be working weekends when all your friends are off, and off weekdays when they're working nine-to-five. They will be able to live your travels vicariously but few will be able to join you on them, as "free" travel benefits generally extend only to your immediate family. In the first few years of your career you will likely be working all the holidays, including Thanksgiving, Christmas, and the 4th of July. You may miss weddings, birthdays, and special events. It will be difficult to make plans more than a month in advance, and even then it will be at the whim of airline schedule changes. Your husband, wife, or significant other may not be able to accept your being gone for days (and nights) at a time. Pets become an unfair burden that someone else must take care of. And you may have to move to a new and strange city, far from your family and friends. Although this may sound severe, it's not much different than starting a new job with any company. The longer you stay with a company, the more seniority you will gain, and the more predictable your schedule will become.

The most important things you will need for the flight attendant job are flexibility and a positive attitude

The airline industry thrives on change, and you must be able to flow with the changes on a constant basis. If you like the routine of a nine-to-five job, this career is not for you. Everything here is non-routine.

At this point, you must ask yourself, "Am I ready for this?" This job will either provide for the most exciting career of your life, or the most disruptive event in your lifestyle. It all depends on the attitude you bring to the job. Even though you may eventually have a somewhat normal work schedule, air travel is dependent on various uncontrollable factors, such as weather, equipment breakdown, and the human factors of illness and work stoppage. With a snowstorm in the Mid-West, your layover in Hawaii could become a layover in Des Moines. Your plans to get married this weekend could be dashed by an air traffic controller strike in Paris. You must be flexible and positive during all of this, as your passengers will have enough inflexibility and negativity for everyone they come in contact with. Since they're locked in an aircraft with you for hours, you're the one to whom they'll be complaining. You must convince them that things aren't so bad after all, and that they should fly again on your airline. The flight attendants are the company personnel with whom the passengers will spend the most time, and they can make the most lasting impression of the airline upon the customers. As a matter of fact, flight attendants are the single most responsible factor for repeat business, the bread and butter of the airline industry. For this reason, flight attendants should be considered very important employees in the company.

> This job will either provide for the most exciting career of your life, or the most disruptive event in your lifestyle

✈ CAREER BENEFITS

If you are able to be flexible and accept change, this career opens up unlimited possibilities. You may travel on your own carrier for free, or close to it. Other airlines will give you fifty, seventy-five, even ninety percent off the regular price of their tickets, and you will be entitled to discounts on hotels and rental cars. These benefits may extend to your parents, spouse, children, and in some cases brothers, sisters, and friends. You will see parts of the United States and world that some people only dream about, and see them on a regular basis. While your friends are shopping at the local malls, you'll be shopping in Paris and Hong Kong. You can ski mid-week when the prices are lower and there are no lift lines. You can ski the Alps! You can shop in Rome and dine in Paris. You will think of boarding a plane and going somewhere the same way other people will think of getting on a city bus and going downtown. You can usually schedule yourself a week or two off from work every month, in addition to your annual vacation. (Some nine-to-fivers only get 1 week of vacation a year!) With seniority, you can schedule your flights so that you can return to college, operate your own business, or travel the world even more. The

> While your friends are shopping at the local malls, you'll be shopping in Paris, Rome, or Hong Kong

opportunities are limited only by your imagination. Plus, you will work with, and come into contact with some of the most diverse and interesting people and cultures in the world. In addition, most carriers offer comprehensive medical and dental insurance, as well as supplemental life insurance at a low cost. These plans are also available to your spouse and children. Nearly all airlines offer retirement plans (with travel benefits!) for employees who have completed a minimum number of years with their respective companies.

✈ TYPES OF AIRLINES

Scheduled: The bulk of the nation's airlines are scheduled airlines, including the smaller "commuter" airlines. This means they publish regular flight schedules, with scheduled in-flight service to the general public. These types of tickets may be purchased up to the time of departure. United, Northwest, and American Airlines are examples of scheduled airlines.

Charter: A charter flight consists of an aircraft that has been contracted to fly from one city to another – usually by a third party. As an example, a Minneapolis tour company will charter an aircraft to fly from Minneapolis to Miami each Friday during the winter months. Minneapolis travel agents and tour companies will then sell the available seats to groups or individuals until the aircraft is filled. Tickets are not sold at the airport, and have to be purchased in advance of the departure date. Passengers can only fly on the charter they're booked on, and cannot transfer their tickets to a scheduled flight. The party that organizes the charter flight also determines the type of in-flight foods and beverages to be served.

FAA safety requirements are the same for charter aircraft as for the scheduled flights. Although charter flights have ticketing restrictions, they are usually offered at prices well below the fares of scheduled flights. Charter flights may operate over regularly scheduled routes, or over routes chosen by the booking party's needs. While many scheduled airlines also charter their aircraft, a charter airline flies only

Although charter flights have ticketing restrictions, they usually offer prices well below the fares of scheduled flights

McDonnell Douglas DC9 *(Narrowbody)*

McDonnell Douglas MD80 *(Narrowbody)*

McDonnell Douglas DC10 *(Widebody)*

Boeing 727 *(Narrowbody)*

Boeing 757 *(Narrowbody)*

Boeing 747 *(Widebody)*

Airbus A320 *(Narrowbody)*

Commuter

charter flights. Evergreen, MGM Grand Air, and Tower Air are examples of charter airlines.

Corporate: Many large corporations, such as IBM, 3M, or Exxon, will own aircraft for the purpose of flying their executives from place to place. These jets may be as small as a Cessna, or as large as a Boeing 727. One or more flight attendants may be present on these jets, depending upon the size. Their work schedules are usually "on-call" or stand-by, as they must be ready when the jet is needed. In addition to their in-flight safety duties, corporate flight attendants may also be required to procure or order the food and supplies needed for every flight. Height restrictions may be stricter, due to the low ceilings of the smaller planes. As most corporate flight attendant recruiters prefer experienced flight attendants, no attempt has been made to list corporate airlines in this guide.

✈ THE APPLICATION PROCESS

In today's airline environment, the competition is fierce. New applicants need to be better prepared than ever. You must do your homework!

The year I was hired as a flight attendant, my airline received one hundred thousand applications, interviewed ten thousand applicants, and hired one thousand. Translated into simpler terms, only one of every hundred applicants was hired.

This was in 1976, when the airlines were undergoing a hiring boom. In today's airline environment, with qualified and experienced flight attendants entering the job market from defunct and bankrupt airlines, the competition is even fiercer. New applicants, therefore, need to be better prepared than ever. You must do your homework!

Take the time to look through the airline listings in the back of this guide, and narrow your choices down to the airlines which you believe you would like to work for. This can be based on personal preference, the routes the airline flies, the flight attendant domiciles, or the carrier's growth potential.

Don't apply for a flight attendant job with an airline whose qualifications you don't meet. If you're 6' 2" and Global Airlines has a height maximum of 6', don't send in an application hoping they'll make an exception because you're such a wonderful person. The first application screening process will look for these variances, and your application will be tossed out before anyone reads further. And

Airlines are most interested in your character

They will be looking at any jobs you've held, your education, and what additional attempts you have made to better yourself

by all means don't lie or exaggerate the facts on your application, hoping to win them over in the interview. If caught, you will not be considered, no matter how innocent the lie. Now, if Global Airlines requires you to be 21 and you are six months shy of that date, state it as that. Knowing you'll possibly be 21 by the time you complete training will cause many airlines to select you for an interview if you meet their other selection criteria.

Once you have narrowed down your list of potential airlines, send for applications using the addresses shown in the listings. Some airlines may require you to send a self-addressed stamped envelope (SASE), which they will use to return an application to you. If the airline requires a resume, have a professional looking resume ready, and attach a cover letter. Your cover letter should be enthusiastic, sincere, personal, and explain why you chose this carrier over the others. The resume should contain: the position desired, professional experience, education, talents, abilities, and languages spoken. All of this should fit on no more than a single page. For the airlines which don't require a resume, the choice is yours whether to send one or not. Some airlines look at them, while others discard them. In the initial inquiry, many airlines are only looking for an address to send an application to.

Fill out the application legibly and neatly—preferably printing or typing. Illegible or hastily scribbled applications will get rejected first.

Airlines are most interested in your character. They will be looking at what type of jobs you've held, how long you've been in each, and your reasons for leaving. They will look at your education, and what additional attempts you have made to improve yourself. For this reason, along with your regular job and education, list everything you've done that might be applicable to the job. List outside activities such as volunteer or charity work, awards or special honors you've received, first aid or CPR courses you have taken, etc. Emphasize public contact experience you may have had. If you know anyone who works for the airline you're applying for, or who is a flight attendant for another airline, list them in the "references" section of the application. (Going out on a date with a flight attendant does not constitute a reference! They have to know you well enough to put their professional reputation on the line for you.) Otherwise, save all other references for your interview.

Follow any special instructions, such as returning the application by mail, or bringing it to the interview. Attach photos only if requested. It's best to keep a log of applications you mail, as you may need to reapply again in six months. Resumes may be kept, returned, or discarded.

Talk to employees who work for the carriers you're interested in; try to learn as much as possible about the airlines you're applying for

Once you've mailed your application, you've done the most you can do. Some airlines will confirm receipt of your application, others may not contact you at all. Most airlines will send a note informing you they're not hiring at the present time, but will retain your application for a specified amount of time. Don't try calling or stopping by the local office of the airline to monitor the hiring progress. The people you will be speaking to are far removed from the selection process, and are much too busy to be bothered by the thousands of applicants seeking the flight attendant job.

If a prospective airline is aware that you understand the job and its duties, then you're that much further ahead

While you're waiting to be scheduled for an interview, what can you do? Now is the time to be doing more homework. Talk to employees who work for the carriers you're interested in; try to learn as much as possible about the airlines you're applying for. Follow the business section of newspapers and magazines for news stories on the industry. Enroll in classes which might prove helpful toward getting the job, such as foreign languages, psychology, sociology, geography, public relations, or philosophy. If a prospective airline is aware that you understand the job and its duties, and don't think (as most people do) that it entails just serving coffee to movie stars on their way to Paris, then you're that much further ahead. The initiative you show in taking these courses will reflect well upon your sense of responsibility during the interview, and will set you apart from the thousands who follow.

✈ HOW TO SHINE IN THE INTERVIEW

Many successful applicants prepare for interviews with their airlines of choice by attending interviews with airlines they have no intention of working for, just for practice

The interviewing process for the position of flight attendant is like no other interview you've ever had. Many successful applicants prepare for interviews with their airlines of choice by attending interviews with airlines they have no intention of working for, just for practice. During the interviewing process, most airlines will start with a road show or "cattle call". A large hall will be rented and groups of applicants will be given an overview of the airline and its job requirements. Then small groups of applicants may be taken before a panel of interviewers. Further interviews may be given at that time, or applicants may be notified of follow-up interviews by phone or mail. The second and third interviews may consist of groups of applicants meeting with a panel of interviewers, a single applicant meeting with a panel, or a one-on-one interview. Usually you will be sent a pass to travel on your prospective airline to interview in their training city. If you don't live near a city your airline flies to, you'll have to pay your own way to get to the closest city where the airline operates.

So what makes these interviews so different? The fact is, the interviewers already know your personal history—it's on your application, which has been pre-screened prior to your arrival. What the interviewers want to find out about you is your character; How do you handle stress? How well do you work as

What the interviewers want to find out about you is your character: how do you handle stress?

a team player? How do you take direction? Are your social graces sufficient to fulfill the requirements of the job? These are the most important criteria toward which the focus of the interview will be shifted. Therefore, the interviewers are not necessarily going to ask you about your last job. They're going to put you in situations and see how you get yourself out of them. For instance, in your group of applicants, you may be asked to stand up on a stage and sing the company's slogan, or invent a new one. They may give you an object, perhaps a pen or paper clip, and instruct you to sell it to the rest of the group. Many will give you in-flight problem situations, for role-playing, and evaluate how you handle them. They want to see how well you "think on your feet". The pressure will be on you to perform, as there are no right or wrong responses. If you list a foreign language on your application, someone will test you, so you had better know more than "Buenos Dias"!

During the entire interview process, consider yourself "on stage". It's not unusual for an airline to be evaluating you as you're waiting to be called into a session. It's a common practice for one of your fellow applicants to be a company employee working undercover. (Some airlines even go so far as to ask the working crew how you behaved on the flight in.) They will be observing you to see how you get along with the others. Are you friendly and talkative, or are you shy and keep to yourself? Your posture and how you sit, walk, and talk will all be checked. This information may be reported before you enter the interviewer's office. You will

You may be asked to stand up on a stage and sing the company's slogan

Always be as upbeat and positive as possible

always want to be on guard. Be friendly, talkative, and sincerely interested in the people around you. Don't criticize the company, or any other airlines for that matter. Always be as upbeat and positive as possible. Interview attire is important also. A smartly tailored suit which is clean and pressed will give you a more businesslike appearance than a trendy or extreme outfit. Avoid wearing too much make-up, applying just enough to enhance your natural features. It's a fallacy to believe that airlines are only looking for people who look like fashion models. Actually it's the overall person they now hire. Age, weight, height, and appearance standards have been relaxed over the years, making this career available to a larger cross-section of the public. Even so, you should put your best appearance forward. Neat, recently trimmed hair (most beard wearers will be asked to shave if hired), clean hands and manicured nails (nail-biters seldom get hired), clear complexion, and a slim, well proportioned figure are very important for both sexes.

A lot has been said lately on the subject of weight requirements. Recent lawsuits against airlines by older flight attendants who were still required to maintain their hiring weight well into their later years, have been settled in favor of the flight attendants. Now airlines will simply say that weight must be "in proportion to height," as opposed to strictly adhered-to weight charts. It will, however, improve your chances at the interview if you display a figure in good physical condition.

The appearance criteria may be very subjective. Every airline looks for a differ-

A smartly tailored suit which is clean and pressed will give you a more businesslike appearance than a trendy or extreme outfit

Each company has a different interpretation of what will fulfill their needs

It's not unusual for an applicant to be turned down by an airline one day, and hired by another the next

ent type of person. Some want the all-American look, others want the sophisticate. Still others will want the characteristics most traditionally associated with the regions in which they operate. Each company, and each interviewer for that company has a different interpretation of what will fullfill their needs. It's not unusual for an applicant to be turned down by an airline one day, and hired by another the next. One friend of mine was turned down three separate times by the same major carrier, was finally hired by them on the fourth try, and now has over ten years seniority. Perseverance is the key to success. If you are turned down by an airline, you will seldom be informed of the reason(s) why. Simply accept the loss, move on, and try them again at a later date. I remember at my final interview, we were all sitting around guessing which applicants would most likely get the job. The ones we all agreed upon as "definitely" getting the job, were never hired. Many of us were amazed that we were chosen instead!

You will want to bring to your interview the following items:

- Social security card
- Passport
- A copy of your birth certificate
- Copies of your resume
- A copy of the information needed on the application
- Letters of reference
- Alien registration & work permit (non- U.S citizen)
- Pen
- Watch

✈ CONGRATULATIONS, YOU'RE HIRED!

APPLICATION APPROVED

You may hear at the interview, or you may be notified weeks later by mail that your chosen airline has selected you. They will usually send you a large information packet with a basic home study course to get you started, along with the paperwork necessary for beginning a new job. Included in the package will be a listing of the 3-letter airport codes for the cities your new airline flies to. You will need to begin memorizing these before you commence training, as it's usually the first test given. Many of these codes are easy to remember, such as DAY (Dayton), PIT (Pittsburgh), BOS (Boston), and MAD (Madrid). Others can be very confusing, such as FCO (Rome), BNA (Nashville), TXL (Berlin) and CVG (Cincinnati). Some airlines will terminate your employment and send you home if you don't pass this first test.

Training is held in the airlines' home city or hub, and most airlines provide lodging for trainees (only two airlines currently charge their trainees to go through training: Family Airlines and Trans World Airlines). Some will begin paying your salary when you start training, some when you complete it. Others will only pay you a *per diem* for food and expenses. (Check the listings in this guide for these individual situations.) Nevertheless, you should come to training with sufficient money for food

Training is held in the airlines' home city or hub, and most airlines provide lodging for trainees

The FAA requires flight attendants to be on board for one reason only, and that is passenger safety

The U.S. Government requires you to be fully trained in safety for each type of aircraft your company operates

and expenses for the three to six weeks duration of training. Pack enough clothing for the duration, also. Business attire is required while in training. You will usually share a room with one, two, or three other trainees.

During the entire time you're in training, and for six months to a year afterward, you will be on probation. This means the airline can fire you for any minor infraction of the rules. Even in airlines with a flight attendant union, full union representation does not commence until you complete the probationary period. The pressure is on for you to be at your best the entire time you are in training. As in the interview process, you will be watched constantly in order to further evaluate your performance, and company spies may again be used.

The general flying public holds the belief that a flight attendant is only on board an aircraft to serve coffee and food. But, as far as the Federal Aviation Administration (FAA) is concerned, meal services and airline public relations are secondary duties for flight attendants. The FAA requires flight attendants to be on board for one reason only, and that is passenger safety. Flight attendants have been called upon to render first-aid for cuts, bruises, burns, choking, and air-sickness, as well as broken bones. There have been instances of flight attendants assisting with childbirth on some flights. The U.S. Government requires you to be fully trained in safety for each type of aircraft your company operates. You will be forbidden to work on an aircraft you haven't been trained and tested on. Every year you

The lives of the passengers and crew alike can depend on the training of the flight attendants

will be re-tested, and failure can mean loss of duty time, and/or your job. You will need to know the type, number, location and use of the fire fighting equipment on board, including the newly installed smoke hoods. Competence is also required in the operation of all emergency exits and evacuation techniques. Basic first-aid, CPR and oxygen administration, and anti-hijacking training will also be included.

To achieve certification by the FAA, every airline must demonstrate that its crews can evacuate an entire aircraft full of passengers in ninety seconds or less. The lives of the passengers and crew alike can depend on the training of the flight attendants. Your airline, therefore, will concentrate heavily on this area. You will be tested constantly on this information, and you must be proficient in all of it to complete training and begin flying.

The FAA requires you to carry a flashlight at all times while on duty, so bring one to training. The "Mini-Maglite™" type has become the preferred flashlight for flight attendants. The Emergency Procedures Manual (EPM) your airline issues to you is also required equipment. This manual serves as your constant guide to company rules, regulations, the handling of unusual situations, and emergency procedures. You can be fined five hundred dollars if an FAA spot check finds you without your flashlight or EPM. A reliable, working watch of a conservative style is also a necessity.

You will be tested constantly on safety information

At the completion of training you will be fitted for your uniform and accessories. You will, in most cases, be expected to purchase your first uniform, though some

You may be given a choice of cities from which you'll begin and end all your flights, or one may be chosen for you

This will be your *home base station*, or *domicile*

Many flight attendants and pilots commute from the cities they live in, to their respective domiciles

airlines will split the cost with you. The average six hundred dollar cost is deducted from your paychecks over the first year of employment. All replacement uniform items are generally paid for by the airline.

You may be given a choice of cities from which you'll begin and end all your flights, or one may be chosen for you by your airline. This will be your *home base station*, or *domicile*. Some airlines have only one domicile for flight attendants, others have as many as twelve. Generally you will be required to remain at your domicile for a set period of time (usually six months) before you can put in a request to transfer to another. Your transfer request will be processed in seniority order. If you're not senior enough for a particular base, or there are no openings there, your request will be denied. Many flight attendants and pilots commute from the cities they live in, to their respective domiciles. My airline has New York-based flight attendants commuting from as far away as Hawaii and Israel. Many commuters will share a "commuter apartment" in the domicile for use when they are spending a night or two between trips. All commuting is done at your own expense, and is not considered an excuse for not making your assigned working flight on time. If you are on *reserve*, you will have to live in your base city during the days you are on call, as you may be given only an hour's notice to appear for a flight.

Airlines look at dependability very closely. As an aircraft is unable to depart if it's not fully staffed, flight attendant absence or tardiness can be very costly to

You should be prepared for relocating when you enter training, keeping in mind the potential cost factors of moving to a new city

hundreds of passengers, as well as to your airline. Excessive incidents of illness, tardiness, or missed flights can lead to discipline and/or dismissal.

After training, you may be given time to return home before starting work in your new city, or you may start work right away. You should be prepared for this when you enter training, keeping in mind the potential cost factors of moving to a new city. You may share an apartment in your new city with the friends you made while in training, or move in with family or friends. Your flight schedule will make it easier for you, as you and your roommates may seldom be in the apartment at the same time. Some airlines allow you travel privileges when you complete training, others when you complete your probationary period. Again, this period of probation is a time when you must be extra diligent. Any infraction of the rules, such as missing a flight, showing up late, etc., can be cause for immediate dismissal.

✈ FLIGHT SCHEDULING

Flight attendants are restricted in the number of hours they can fly each month. *Flight hours* are considered the time from when the aircraft leaves the airport gate (*block out*) to when it arrives at the next airport gate (*block in*). Your salary will be based on block hours every month, with the minimum number of hours varying with each airline. You will see each airline's salary in the listings section, based upon minimum flight requirements.

"What a job!" you say, after looking through the listings, "I only have to work seventy-five hours every month!" This is a common misconception your friends and passengers will share. In actuality, you will be away from home two hundred and fifty to three hundred hours per month, but only get flight pay for seventy-five. Time spent on the ground during pre-flight, boarding, and deplaning is time during which you will be paid only *per diem*. You may also receive a per diem for the time you are away from home, to help with your food expenses.

In most cases, when you complete training, you will be assigned to one of the *domiciles* your airline has established for its flight attendants. Again, this may be a city of your choosing or it may be the city of the airline's choice.

January

Sun	Mon	Tue	Wed	Thu	Fri	Sat
	1	2	3	4	5	6
7	8	9	10	11	12	13
14	15	16	17	18	19	20
21	22	23	24	25	26	27
28	29	30	31			

Some airlines even allow you to split your month with another flight attendant

You will be assigned a *reserve line of time* for your first month. This means you will be on call, and must be packed and ready to leave on a moment's notice. You may be waiting at home, or you may be required to wait in full uniform at the airport. When another flight attendant calls in sick, is late, or is otherwise unable to work a flight, a *reserve* will be called to fill the opening. The FAA also dictates the number of flight attendants that must be aboard a given aircraft, and the aircraft cannot depart until this number is met. Your ability as a reserve to make it to the airport on time may determine if a flight filled with people leaves on schedule or not.

The longer you work for an airline, the more *seniority* you will gain. This seniority will eventually be sufficient to enable you to hold a *line of time*. Each month a listing of scheduled flights is distributed to the flight attendants. You will choose which flights you wish to work in order of preference. You may choose your specific trips because of the length of the trip, the length and/or location of layovers, the days off from duty or the number of days away from home. These trips may consist of multi-day *flight pairings*, or *turnarounds*, which depart and return on the same day with no overnight. These pairings are usually spread throughout the month, and may be 2-on-3-off (two days on duty followed by three days off) 3-on-2-off, back-to-back (flights scheduled one after the other, allowing only minimum rest between each), or any combination of trips, short or long. The FAA once again regulates a part of this, as it has minimum standards for *legal rest* from duty. When bids close, all bid requests are tallied in seniority order, and you are *awarded* your schedule for the following month. If you are not senior enough to *hold a line*, you will be scheduled into the reserve pool. Most reserve lines also have scheduled days off, when you will not be required to sit by the phone. Many airlines also allow reserves to utilize a beeper – at their own expense, of course.

If you are holding a line, some airlines allow trading of flights to arrange your schedule more to your liking. Some airlines even allow you to split your month with another flight attendant. This is known as *job sharing*. (This works extremely well for flight attendants who are also parents or students.)

Seniority is your whole life in the airlines. It dictates what trips you fly, what position you work on the aircraft, who gets a hotel room first, when you take your vacation, and when you get pay raises. For this reason, switching airlines in mid-career can be very difficult, as you must begin at the bottom of the seniority list at your new airline.

Seniority is your whole life in the airlines

✈ A TYPICAL THREE DAY TRIP

While each airline has service nuances which differ from the others, the routine of the job is basically the same. In a nutshell, here's a typical three day trip:

You begin by reporting for duty at your domicile airport, in full uniform and fully packed, at least one hour prior to your scheduled flight departure. You will meet with your fellow crew members, some of whom you may be meeting for the first time. A crew briefing usually follows, and may include *bidding* for a working position on the aircraft. You will board the aircraft approximately forty-five minutes prior to departure. Once on board you will ensure that your gear is properly stowed, and you will check that all emergency equipment is in working condition. In training you learned the locations and operation of all the emergency equipment for all the different types of aircraft your airline operates. The absence of some emergency equipment can prevent an aircraft from departing until it is replaced, so this check is very important. Next you'll check food and supplies to ensure you have enough for the passenger load. At a flight altitude of thirty-thousand feet there is no place to get the things you need! Next is the boarding of the passengers, whom you will assist in seating. Then the door is closed, and you will complete your safety requirements by

At a flight altitude of thirty thousand feet there is no place to get the things you need!

demonstrating the safety equipment and exits to your passengers. Finally, you will visually check to ensure that all passengers have complied with safety requirements. Then it's time to take your jumpseat for take-off.

When you reach cruise altitude, you will serve drinks, followed by a meal. When you have finished serving the last row of passengers, you will begin picking up the finished trays and glasses at the front row. Federal Air regulations prohibit loose articles in the cabin during landing. As you're on board to ensure that FAA Regulations (FAR's) are maintained, everything must be picked up and stowed in its proper place prior to touching down. A final check on your passengers, and you'll buckle up for landing. You assist as the passengers deplane, then may tidy the aircraft when they're gone. New food and supplies are boarded, and the cycle begins again for the next portion, or "leg" of the flight. Some trips may have only one leg a day, others may have as many as seven to ten. You must appear as fresh and friendly on the seventh leg as you did on the first. A workday may range from a few hours to ten to fourteen hour days.

At the end of the day, you and your fellow crew members will take a courtesy bus to your hotel for the night. Hotel rooms are paid for by the airline, but you pay for your own food and beverages, as well as tips for the bus drivers who handle your bags. Your layover can range from six to eight hours, (barely enough time for a good night's sleep) to sixteen to twenty-four hour layovers where you can tour the local area. Multi-day layovers are becoming scarce in these tight-money times. Most crews on layovers of less than twenty-four hours are put up at a hotel near the airport.

The next morning you will accompany the rest of the crew back to the airport to begin again. This day it's a cross-country flight (TransCon) with a more elaborate service, which will keep you busy for the entire flight. During the showing of the in-flight movie, you may have a chance to grab a meal and chat with the passengers and crew. (Yesterday's flight afforded little time for talking with passengers.) This layover is in San Francisco for twenty-one hours, so you'll have time to go out with the crew for dinner at Fishermans' Wharf before turning in for the night.

The next morning, you'll work three legs home, and you'll have the next two days off before reporting for your next flight. In the preceding days you've covered six thousand miles, served nine meals, been gone from home for sixty hours, and been paid for fifteen flight hours plus sixty hours of per diem. Four more of these three-day trips, and you will have completed your month.

Your pay check for this month is calculated on the next page.

> A layover in San Francisco for twenty-one hours will afford you time to go out with the crew for dinner at Fishermans' Wharf before turning in for the night

Using United Airlines 1992 rates of pay as an example, here is what your pay check for the month might look like:

5 trips
x 15 flight hours per trip
= 75 flight hours
75 hours – 65 hour monthly rate
= 10 hours overtime
60 hours away from home per trip
x 5 trips
=300 hrs.

Base rate	*1101.00*
Overtime (10 X 16.94)	*169.40*
Per diem (300 X 1.55)	*465.00*
	$1,335.40

In addition, some airlines will have additional rates of pay, for such things as holidays, birthdays, night pay, "over water" pay, "lead" flight attendant (also known as "A" flight attendant, number one, service manager, or purser) and/or for speaking a foreign language. These rates of pay, in addition to periodic raises, will vary from airline to airline, depending on the contractual working agreements of each. Salary increases usually commence after six months to one year of service.

Most airlines also prefer to hire from within when they have job openings for in-flight supervisors, trainers and instructors. In addition, if you have the required education, advancement into the pilot or corporate structure is also possible. The schooling for these positions is done on your own, outside of the airline.

Most airlines also prefer to hire from within when they have job openings for in-flight supervisors, trainers and instructors

✈ YOUR FUTURE IN THE SKIES

The job of airline flight attendant can be the most interesting and challenging job you ever acquire. If at first you don't succeed in landing the position, keep trying, for persistence pays off in this field. Some applicants may opt to start in another position with an airline – the so-called "ground" jobs, transferring to a flight attendant position when it becomes available. Ground jobs include ticket agent, customer service agent, reservations, office staff, sky cap, sales, baggage handler... to name a few. After a few years of flying, some flight attendants opt to transfer into a managerial or supervisory position within their companies.

You'll never forget the experiences you will have had, the places you will see, or the people you will meet

Whether you are a flight attendant for a few years, or make it a career, you'll never forget the experiences you will have, the places you will see or the people you will meet. After nearly two decades of flying, I consider my job of flight attendant to have been the best choice I ever made—opening up opportunities I never dreamt existed. I'm looking forward to another two decades in the industry. Perhaps we'll have the opportunity to work together on a flight, and I can listen to all the experiences you've had.

✈ VOCABULARY

ARM- The act of positioning an emergency slide or exit in the emergency-ready mode.

BASE STATION- A station at which flight attendants are based. Also called a domicile.

BIDDING- The process of selecting a flight schedule from a master listing or "bid package," in order of preference. Actual schedule is then determined in seniority order.

BLOCK TO BLOCK- The period of time from when the aircraft leaves the airport gate to when it arrives at the next airport gate. Also known as block hours.

BULKHEAD- A wall separating cabins in an aircraft.

BUSINESS CLASS- A mid-range cabin priced between coach and first class.

CABIN- The interior of an aircraft, where passengers are seated.

CHARTER FLIGHT- A non-scheduled flight which may operate over regularly serviced routes, or over routes chosen by the booking party's needs.

CHECK IN TIME- The time at which a flight attendant is scheduled to arrive at the airport for duty.

COACH- The rear-most passenger section of the cabin. Also known as tourist class.

COCKPIT- The pilots' compartment in the front of the aircraft. Also known as the flight deck.

CONTRACT- A working agreement between an airline and the members of a labor organization, which specifies hours of service, rates of pay, etc.

CPR- Emergency life support procedure that consists of the recognition and treatment of the absence of breathing and circulation.

CRAF- Civil Reserve Air Fleet. Military usage of commercial aircraft for transport of personnel.

CREW KIT- Suitcase or bag used by the flight attendants and pilots for personal items.

CREW SCHEDULING- Crew planning and scheduling office.

DEADHEAD- To travel on company business in a non-working capacity. You may ride as a passenger to get to your flight assignment as part of your trip pairing.

DOMICILE- A station at which flight attendants are based. Also called base station.

ENGINEER- The pilot who is third in command, and maintains the electrical and mechanical systems of the aircraft. Some aircraft have no engineer.

EPM- Emergency Procedures Manual, issued by airlines to flight attendants in training. The FAA requires you to carry your EPM with you at all times while on duty.

ETA- Estimated time of arrival.
ETD- Estimated time of departure.

EVACUATION- The procedure of deplaning passengers from an aircraft in the timeliest manner possible during an emergency.

EXTRA SECTION- An additional flight added to a scheduled route in order to accommodate additional passengers.

FAA – Federal Aviation Administration.

FAR- Federal Aviation Regulation.

FERRY FLIGHT- Delivery of an aircraft without passengers to a destination. Flight attendants may or may not accompany the aircraft.

FIRST CLASS- Premier class of service, usually in the forward section of the cabin.

FIRST OFFICER- The second-in-command pilot on a flight.

FLIGHT ATTENDANT- Also known as purser, cabin attendant, steward/ess, crew member. Attends to passengers' comfort and safety.

FLIGHT PAIRINGS- Sequence of flights which make up each "trip".

FUSELAGE- The main body of the aircraft, excluding wings, tail and engines.

GALLEY- The area on the aircraft where food is stored and prepared.

GATE- Passenger boarding door of airport.

HOLD A LINE- To work a scheduled sequence of flight pairings.

HOLDING- Waiting- as in waiting to be cleared to land.

JETWAY- An enclosed passageway through which passengers move from airport to aircraft.

JOB SHARING- Splitting of bid month schedule with another flight attendant.

LAYOVER- A scheduled rest period away from domicile.

LEGAL REST- Minimum rest time required after flight time. Some is required by the FAA, some is required by contractual agreements.

LINE OF TIME- A monthly sequence of flight pairings.

NON-ROUTINE- Not part of a regular schedule.

PER DIEM- Daily allowance for reimbursement of out-of-pocket expenses. (Latin for "by the day").

PREFLIGHT- The act of checking emergency equipment and supplies on an aircraft prior to passenger boarding.

RAMP- The cement area adjacent to the terminal which is for aircraft parking, loading and unloading.

RESERVE- A flight attendant who has no regular schedule, but is on call.

RESERVE LINE OF TIME- Monthly schedule for flight attendants on reserve. May show scheduled days off.

SENIORITY- A flight attendant's precedence over others of the same rank by reason of a longer span of service.

STAND-BY- A flight attendant on reserve, who is required to wait either at home or at the airport for an immediate flight assignment. Also, a passenger who has no reservation, but is waiting for an open seat.

TAXI- Aircraft movement on the ground.

TRANS CON- Cross country or coast-to-coast flight.

TURBULENCE- Irregular movement of the aircraft caused by changes in atmospheric air currents.

TURNAROUND FLIGHT- Any flight pairing which originates from and returns to the same city on the same day.

✈ COMMON AIRPORT CODES

ABE	Allentown, PA
ABQ	Albuquerque, NM
ACY	Atlantic City, NJ
ALB	Albany, NY
ANC	Anchorage, AK
AOO	Altoona, PA
ATL	Atlanta, GA
ATW	Appleton, WI
AUS	Austin, TX
BDL	Hartford, CT
BGM	Binghamton, NY
BIL	Billings, MT
BGR	Bangor, ME
BNA	Nashville, TN
BOI	Boise, ID
BOS	Boston,MA
BUF	Buffalo, NY
BUR	Burbank,CA
BWI	Baltimore, MD
CAE	Columbia, SC
CHS	Charleston, SC
CKB	Clarksburg, KY
CLE	Cleveland, OH
CLT	Charlotte, NC
CMH	Columbus, OH
CPR	Casper, WY
CVG	Cincinnati, OH
DAL	Dallas, TX – Love Field
DAY	Dayton, OH
DCA	Washington DC – National
DEN	Denver, CO
DFW	Dallas/Ft.Worth, TX
DSM	Des Moines, IA
DTW	Detroit, MI
DUJ	Dubois, PA
EEN	Keene, NH
ELP	El Paso, TX
EWN	New Bern,NC
EWR	Newark, NJ

FAT	Fresno, CA
FLL	Ft.Lauderdale, FL
FLO	Florence, SC
FNT	Flint, MI
FWA	Ft.Wayne, IN
GEG	Spokane, WA
GON	New London, CT
GSP	Greenville/Spartanburg, SC
HNL	Honolulu, HI
HOU	Houston, TX-Hobby
IAD	Washington DC-Dulles
IAH	Houston, TX
ICT	Wichita, KS
IND	Indianapolis, IN
IPT	Williamsport, PA
JAN	Jackson, MS
JAX	Jacksonville, FL
JFK	New York, NY- JFK
JST	Johnstown, PA
LAS	Las Vegas, NV
LAX	Los Angeles,CA
LEX	Lexington, KY
LGA	New York, NY-La Guardia
LGB	Long Beach, CA
LHR	London – Heathrow, England
LNS	Lansing, MI
LYH	Lynchburg, VA
MCI	Kansas City, MO
MCN	Macon, GA
MCO	Orlando, FL
MDT	Middletown, PA
MDW	Chicago, IL-Midway
MEM	Memphis, TN
MHT	Manchester, NH
MIA	Miami, FL
MKE	Milwaukee, WI
MSN	Madison, WI
MSP	Minneapolis/St.Paul, MN
MSY	New Orleans, LA
OAK	Oakland, CA
OKC	Oklahoma City, OK
OMA	Omaha, NE

ONT	Ontario, CA
ORD	Chicago, IL-O'Hare
ORF	Norfolk, VA
ORH	Worcester, MA
PBI	West Palm Beach, FL
PDX	Portland, OR
PHF	Hampton, VA
PHL	Philadelphia, PA
PHX	Phoenix, AZ
PIT	Pittsburgh, PA
PNE	N. Philidelphia Airport, PA
PSP	Palm Springs, CA
PVD	Providence, RI
PWM	Portland, ME
RDD	Redding, CAS
RDU	Raleigh/Durham, NC
RIC	Richmond, VA
RNO	Reno, NV
ROC	Rochester, NY
SAC	Sacramento, CA
SAN	San Diego, CA
SAT	San Antonio, TX
SAV	Savannah, GA
SBY	Salisbury, MD
SCE	State College, NY
SDF	Louisville, KY
SEA	Seattle, WA
SFO	San Francisco, CA
SJC	San Jose, CA
SJU	San Juan, Puerto Rico
SLC	Salt Lake City, UT
SLO	Salem, IL
SMF	Sacramento, CA
SNA	Orange County, CA
STL	St.Louis, MO
STT	St. Thomas, VI
STX	St. Croix, VI
SYR	Syracuse, NY
TPA	Tampa, FL
TUS	Tucson, AZ
YNG	Youngstown, OH

✈ THE AIRLINE LISTINGS

The airline listings are arranged in alphabetical order. You will note that some of the commuter airlines share the same address for applying. Information which is standard between all the airlines is listed in the previous text, and not in the listings. These items are:

- English language requirement.
- Pre-employment drug test.
- Pre-employment physical.
- Weight in proportion to height.
- High School graduation or G.E.D.
- History of public contact work.

Some of the airlines list their salaries by the hour, while others indicate theirs by the month. The hourly rate may be determined by dividing the monthly rate by the minimum flight hours per month. (e.g. monthly salary of $1050. divided by 75 hours equals $14.00 per hour.) The overtime rate will begin after the monthly minimum hours are reached. When the airline has no overtime rate, the regular hourly rate will apply.

The domicile stations for each airline are also included in the airport/city code page of the text, with the exception of the code NYC. Several airlines will indicate one domicile in New York City, with flights operating out of the LaGuardia (LGA), John F.Kennedy (JFK), and Newark, NJ (EWR) airports.

✈ FINAL NOTES BEFORE TAKE-OFF

America West Airlines is unique in the industry, in that it's employees are not hired for specific job categories, but will instead work many positions. Flight attendant applicants also work as ticket agents, baggage handlers, and reservation agents. For this reason, some of the questions in the AW listing could not be answered with "yes" or "no" answers.

Aloha Airlines, TWA/TWExpress and COMAIR/Delta Connection declined to be included in this publication, as a matter of company policies.

I hope this guide will prove to be your greatest asset in landing your career in the skies. I wish you the best of luck in aquiring the position, and hope all your flights are full of interesting passengers. Please write me if I may be of any further assistance, or to pass on your comments and suggestions for possible inclusion in the next issue of *THE FLIGHT ATTANDENT CAREER GUIDE*. I would really love to hear your stories! Write me at P.O.Box 6455, Delray Beach, FL 33484-6455.

✈ AIR MICRONESIA

Airline type: Scheduled.
Resume required? Yes. **SASE required with application?** No. **Application retained:** 6 months. **Fee for applying:** None. **How many interviews/ what type?** Two or three - group/private. **Transportation to interview paid by airline?** No.

REQUIREMENTS: **Height:** 5' - 6'. **Minimum age:** 20. **Language(s) preferred:** Japanese & Chinese.

SALARY AND EXPENSES: **Base pay/ hours minimum:** $14.85 (80). **Overtime rate:** None. **Per diem:** $1.50 **B-Scale:** None. **Uniform costs:** $850. **Training length/ location:** 6 weeks/ Guam. **Training cost:** None. **Salary earned while in training:** None. **Company paid housing provided?** No. **Domiciles:** Guam. **Flight Attendant Union:** International Association of Machinists.

APPLICATION ADDRESS: Continental Air Micronesia, Personnel Department, P.O.Box 8778-P, Tamuning, GU 96911.

✈ AIRWAYS INTERNATIONAL

Airline type: Scheduled.
Resume required? No. **SASE required with application?** Yes. **Application retained:** 1 year **Fee for applying:** None. **How many interviews/ what type?** One - private. **Transportation to interview paid by airline?** No.

REQUIREMENTS: **Height:** 5'3 - 6'. **Minimum age:** 21. **Language(s) preferred:** None.

SALARY AND EXPENSES: **Base pay/ hours minimum:** $800. (80). **Overtime rate:** $15.00. **Per diem:** $25 per overnite **B-Scale:** None. **Uniform costs:** $100 repaid after probation. **Training length/ location:** 1 week/MIA. **Training cost:** None. **Salary earned while in training:** None. **Company paid housing provided?** No. **Domiciles:** MIA. **Flight Attendant Union:** None.

APPLICATION ADDRESS: Airways International, Attn: Director IFS, P.O.Box 1244, Miami Springs, FL 33266-1244.

✈ AIR WISCONSIN

Airline type: Scheduled.

Resume required? No. **SASE required with application?** Yes. **Application retained:** 1 year **Fee for applying:** $10. **How many interviews/ what type?** Two - group/private. **Transportation to interview paid by airline?** On-line only.

REQUIREMENTS: **Height:** 5'1" - 6'. **Minimum age:** 20. **Language(s) preferred:** None.

SALARY AND EXPENSES: **Base pay/ hours minimum:** $12.50 (68). **Overtime rate:** $12.50. **Per diem:** $1.35 **B-Scale:** None. **Uniform costs:** $700-800. **Training length/ location:** 5 weeks/ATW. **Training cost:** None. **Salary earned while in training:** $25 per day. **Company paid housing provided?** Yes. **Domiciles:** ATW DEN IAD FWA ORD RIC. **Flight Attendant Union:** Association of Flight Attendants.

APPLICATION ADDRESS: Air Wisconsin, Attn: Human Resources, 203 Challenger Drive, Appleton, WI 54915.

✈ ALASKA

Airline type: Scheduled.

Resume required? No. **SASE required with application?** No. **Application retained:** 12 months. **Fee for applying:** None. **How many interviews/ what type?** Three - group/private/private. **Transportation to interview paid by airline?** Yes .

REQUIREMENTS: **Height:** Must pass reach test. **Minimum age:** 21. **Language(s) preferred:** Spanish.

SALARY AND EXPENSES: **Base pay/ hours minimum:** $1050. (65). **Overtime rate:** $18.50. **Per diem:** $1.30 **B-Scale:** Yes. **Uniform costs:** $600. **Training length/ location:** 5 weeks/ SEA. **Training cost:** None. **Salary earned while in training:** $8 per day. **Company paid housing provided?** For non-Seattle residents. **Domiciles:** SEA LGB. **Flight Attendant Union:** Association of Flight Attendants.

APPLICATION ADDRESS: Alaska Airlines, Attn: Flight Attendant Hiring, P.O.Box 68900, Seattle, WA 98168.

✈ USAIR EXPRESS/ALLEGHANY COMMUTER

Airline type: Scheduled.

Resume required? Yes. **SASE required with application?** No. **Application retained:** 12 months. **Fee for applying:** None. **How many interviews/ what type?** Two - group/panel. **Transportation to interview paid by airline?** Yes

REQUIREMENTS: **Height:** None. **Minimum age:** 21. **Language(s) preferred:** None.

SALARY AND EXPENSES: **Base pay/ hours minimum:** $13.26 (65). **Overtime rate:** $13.26. **Per diem:** $25 per overnite **B-Scale:** None. **Uniform costs:** $600. **Training length/ location:** 4 weeks/ RDG. **Training cost:** None. **Salary earned while in training:** Yes, retroactively, after successful completion of training. **Company paid housing provided?** Yes. **Domiciles:** AVP ACY LSP PHL BWI MDT SCE. **Flight Attendant Union:** Association of Flight Attendants.

APPLICATION ADDRESS: USAir Express/Alleghany Commuter, Attn: Doug Smith- Human Resources, 1000 Rosedale Avenue, Middletown, PA 17057-0432.

✈ AMERICAN AIRLINES

Airline type: Scheduled.

Resume required? No. **SASE required with application?** No. **Application retained:** 12 months. **Fee for applying:** $25. **How many interviews/ what type?** One: group. **Transportation to interview paid by airline?** Yes.

REQUIREMENTS: **Height:** 5'1 1/2" - 6. **Minimum age:** 20. **Language(s) preferred:** Japanese, Swedish, Spanish, French, Portugese, German, Italian, Dutch, and other languages.

SALARY AND EXPENSES: **Base pay/ hours minimum:** $16.07 (67). **Overtime rate:** $18.49. **Per diem:** $1.50 **B-Scale:** 9 years. **Uniform costs:** $800 - $1000. **Training length/ location:** 5 1/2 weeks/ DFW. **Training cost:** None. **Salary earned while in training:** None. **Company paid housing provided?** Yes. **Domiciles:** NYC SJU SFO LAX MIA ORD DCA DFW BNA RDU SEA SAN HNL BOS. **Flight Attendant Union:** Association of Professional Flight Attendants.

APPLICATION ADDRESS: American Airlines, P.O.Box 619410, Mail Drop 4125 Dallas-Ft.Worth Airport, TX 75261-9410.

✈ AMERICAN EAGLE SIMMONS

Airline type: Scheduled.

Resume required? No. **SASE required with application?** Yes. **Application retained:** 24 months. **Fee for applying:** None. **How many interviews/ what type?** Two- group/one-on-one. **Transportation to interview paid by airline?** Yes.

REQUIREMENTS: **Height:** 5' - 5'10. **Minimum age:** 19. **Language(s) preferred:** None.

SALARY AND EXPENSES: **Base pay/ hours minimum:** $735. (70 hours). **Overtime rate:** $10.50. **Per diem:** $1.05 hr. **B-Scale:** None. **Uniform costs:** $750-800. **Training length/ location:** 3 1/2 weeks/DFW. **Training cost:** None. **Salary earned while in training:** None. **Company paid housing provided?** Yes. **Domiciles:** ORD DFW MQT. **Flight Attendant Union:** Association of Flight Attendants.

APPLICATION ADDRESS: AMR Eagle Recruitment, MD 4121, P.O.Box 619415, DFW Airport, TX 75261-9415.

✈ AMERICAN TRANS AIR

Airline type: Charter.

Resume required? No. **SASE required with application?** No. **Application retained:** 6 months. **Fee for applying:** None. **How many interviews/ what type?** Two- group/individual. **Transportation to interview paid by airline?** No.

REQUIREMENTS: **Height:** 5'2 - 6'1. **Minimum age:** 18. **Language(s) preferred:** German, French,Portugese, Spanish.

SALARY AND EXPENSES: **Base pay/ hours minimum:** $15. (75). **Overtime rate:** $15. **Per diem:** $1.85 Int'l. $1.15 Dom. **B-Scale:** None. **Uniform costs:** $275-400. **Training length/ location:** 4 weeks/IND. **Training cost:** None. **Salary earned while in training:** $20 per day upon completion. **Company paid housing provided?** Yes. **Domiciles:** IND JFK DTW SFO ORD BOS LAS MCO. **Flight Attendant Union:** Association of Flight Attendants.

APPLICATION ADDRESS: American Trans Air, Attn: Flight Attendant/ Corporate Recruiter, P.O.Box 51609, Indianapolis Int'l. Airport, Indianapolis, IN 46251-0609.

✈ AMERICA WEST

Airline type: Scheduled.
Resume required? No. **SASE required with application?** No. **Application retained:** 6 months. **Fee for applying:** None. **How many interviews/ what type?** Three- group/private/private. **Transportation to interview paid by airline?** Yes, on-line.
REQUIREMENTS: **Height:** 5' - 6'3. **Minimum age:** 21. **Language(s) preferred:** None.
SALARY AND EXPENSES: **Base pay/ hours minimum:** $1050. (75). **Overtime rate:** Varies. **Per diem:** Varies **B-Scale:** None. **Uniform costs:** None. **Training length/ location:** Length varies/Tempe. **Training cost:** None. **Salary earned while in training:** On job only. **Company paid housing provided?** No. **Domiciles:** PHX. **Flight Attendant Union:** None.
APPLICATION ADDRESS: America West Airlines, Attn: Employment Dept., 4000 E Sky Harbor Blvd., Phoenix, AZ 85034.

✈ ATLANTIC SOUTHEAST AIRLINES DELTA CONNECTION

Airline type: Scheduled.
Resume required? No. **SASE required with application?** No. **Application retained:** 6 months. **Fee for applying:** None. **How many interviews/ what type?** Two- group/private. **Transportation to interview paid by airline?** On-line only.
REQUIREMENTS: **Height:** Proportionate. **Minimum age:** 21. **Language(s) preferred:** None.
SALARY AND EXPENSES: **Base pay/ hours minimum:** $980. (75). **Overtime rate:** None. **Per diem:** $16.50 per night **B-Scale:** None. **Uniform costs:** $500. **Training length/ location:** 3 weeks/ATL. **Training cost:** None. **Salary earned while in training:** $20 per day for expenses. **Company paid housing provided?** Yes. **Domiciles:** ATL MCN DFW. **Flight Attendant Union:** Association of Flight Attendants.
APPLICATION ADDRESS: Atlantic Southeast Airlines, Attn: Flight Attendant Recruiter, 100 Hartsfield Centre Parkway, Atlanta, GA 30349.

✈ BRANSON AIR

Airline type: Scheduled.
Resume required? Yes. **SASE required with application?** No.
Application retained: 6 months. **Fee for applying:** None. **How many interviews/ what type?** Two- group/one-on-one.
Transportation to interview paid by airline? No.
REQUIREMENTS: **Height:** 5'2" - 5'9". **Minimum age:** 21.
Language(s) preferred: Itlian, Spanish. **Other:** Must swim. Must pass 3rd class FAA flight physical.
SALARY AND EXPENSES: **Base pay/ hours minimum:** $15-20.
Overtime rate: None. Per diem: $1.70. **B-Scale:** None. **Uniform costs:** None. **Training length/ location:** 2 weeks/Varies.
Training cost: None. **Salary earned while in training:** None given. **Company paid housing provided?** Non-South Florida residents. **Domiciles:** FLL MCI plus others. Flight Attendant Union: None.
APPLICATION ADDRESS: Branson Air, Attn: Dee Buchanan, 2600 NW 62nd Street, Ft. lauderdale, FL 33309.

✈ BUSINESS EXPRESS DELTA CONNECTION

Airline type: Scheduled.
Resume required? Yes, with picture preferred. **SASE required with application?** No. **Application retained:** 12 months. **Fee for applying:** $15. **How many interviews/ what type?** Varies. **Transportation to interview paid by airline?** On-line only.
REQUIREMENTS: **Height:** 5' - 6'. **Minimum age:** 20.
Language(s) preferred: French.
SALARY AND EXPENSES: **Base pay/ hours minimum:** $15,500. (75). **Overtime rate:** None. **Per diem:** Depends on trip length **B-Scale:** No. **Uniform costs:** Varies. **Training length/ location:** Varies. **Training cost:** Expenses only. **Salary earned while in training:** Yes. **Company paid housing provided?** Yes. **Domiciles:** BDL ALB PVD. **Flight Attendant Union:** None.
APPLICATION ADDRESS: Business Express, Attn: Flight Attendant Employment, Hanger 85-172, Bradley Airport, Windsor Locks CT 06096.

✈ CARNIVAL AIR LINES

Airline type: Scheduled.

Resume required? Yes. **SASE required with application?** Yes. **Application retained:** 6 months. **Fee for applying:** None. **How many interviews/ what type?** Two - group/private. **Transportation to interview paid by airline?** No.

REQUIREMENTS: **Height:** 5'2 - 6'1. **Minimum age:** 21. **Language(s) preferred:** French, Spanish.

SALARY AND EXPENSES: **Base pay/ hours minimum:** $1100. (65). **Overtime rate:** None. **Per diem:** $1.30 **B-Scale:** None. **Uniform costs:** $700. **Training length/ location:** 3-4 weeks/FLL. **Training cost:** None. **Salary earned while in training:** $25 per day. **Company paid housing provided?** For out-of-town trainees. **Domiciles:** PHL JFK/EWR FLL/MIA PSE. **Flight Attendant Union:** None.

APPLICATION ADDRESS: Carnival Air Lines, Attn: Human Resources, 1815 Griffin Road Suite 205, Dania, FL 33004.

✈ CCAIR

Airline type: Scheduled.

Resume required? Yes. **SASE required with application?** No. **Application retained:** 6 months. **Fee for applying:** None. **How many interviews/ what type?** Two - private/private. **Transportation to interview paid by airline?** Yes, on-line.

REQUIREMENTS: **Height:** 5'2 - 5'11. **Minimum age:** 21. **Language(s) preferred:** None.

SALARY AND EXPENSES: **Base pay/ hours minimum:** $13.00 (70). **Overtime rate:** $13.00 **Per diem:** $1.15 **B-Scale:** None. **Uniform costs:** Varies. Payroll deducted @ $24 per month. **Training length/ location:** 3 weeks/ CLT. **Training cost:** None. **Salary earned while in training:** $26.00 per day. **Company paid housing provided?** Yes. **Domiciles:** CLT HKY INT PGV. **Flight Attendant Union:** Association of Flight Attendants.

APPLICATION ADDRESS: CCAIR, INC., Flight Attendant Recruiting, 100 Terminal Road, Charlotte, NC 28208.

✈ CONTINENTAL AIRLINES

Airline type: Scheduled.

Resume required? Yes. **SASE required with application?** Yes. **Application retained:** 6 months. **Fee for applying:** $20 (except Hawaii). **How many interviews/ what type?** Three- Group/one-on-one. **Transportation to interview paid by airline?** Yes.

REQUIREMENTS: **Height:** 5' - 6'2 **Min. age:** 20. **Language(s) preferred:** French, German or Spanish,Japanese.

SALARY AND EXPENSES: **Base pay/ hours minimum:** $13.61 (83). **Overtime rate:** $13.61 **Per diem:** $1.15 Domestic $1.60 Intl. **B-Scale:** None. **Uniform costs:** $720. **Training length/ location:** 6 weeks/IAH. **Training cost:** None. **Salary earned while in training:** $105. Per week. **Company paid housing provided?** Yes. **Domiciles:** CLE DEN HNL IAH LAX EWR. **Flight Attendant Union:** International Association of Machinists.

APPLICATION ADDRESS: Continental Airlines, Attn: In-Flight Recruiting, P.O.Box 4748, Houston, TX 77210-4748.

✈ CONTINENTAL EXPRESS

Airline type: Scheduled.

Resume required? Yes. **SASE required with application?** Yes. **Application retained:** 6 months. **Fee for applying:** $20. **How many interviews/ what type?** Three - group/group/private. **Transportation to interview paid by airline?** Yes.

REQUIREMENTS: **Height:** 5' - 5'7. **Minimum age:** 20. **Language(s) preferred:** None.

SALARY AND EXPENSES: **Base pay/ hours minimum:** $13.50 (80). **Overtime rate:** $13.50. **Per diem:** $1.00 **B-Scale:** None. **Uniform costs:** $550. **Training length/ location:** 4 weeks/ HOU. **Training cost:** None. **Salary earned while in training:** $24 per day. **Company paid housing provided?** Yes. **Domiciles:** EWR CLE HOU DEN. **Flight Attendant Union:** None.

APPLICATION ADDRESS: Continental Express, 15333 JFK Blvd. Suite 600, Houston, TX 77032.

✈ CROWN AIRWAYS

Airline type: Scheduled.

Resume required? Yes. **SASE required with application?** No. **Application retained:** 12 months. **Fee for applying:** None. **How many interviews/ what type?** Two- group/private. **Transportation to interview paid by airline?** Yes, space available.

REQUIREMENTS: **Height:** 5'2 - 6'2. **Minimum age:** 19. **Language(s) preferred:** None.

SALARY AND EXPENSES: **Base pay/ hours minimum:** $850. (75). **Overtime rate:** $11.33. **Per diem:** None. **B-Scale:** None. **Uniform costs:** $630. **Training length/ location:** 3 weeks/ PKB. **Training cost:** None. **Salary earned while in training:** $25 per day upon successful completion of training. **Company paid housing provided?** Yes, upon successful completion of training. **Domiciles:** PKB YNG CKB DUJ. **Flight Attendant Union:** None.

APPLICATION ADDRESS: Crown Airways, Flight Attendant Department, 102 Airport Road, Williamstown, WV 26187.

✈ DELTA AIRLINES

Airline type: Scheduled.

Resume required? No. **SASE required with application?** No. **Application retained:** 12 months. **Fee for applying:** No. **How many interviews/ what type?** Three - group/private/private. **Transportation to interview paid by airline?** Yes, on-line.

REQUIREMENTS: **Height:** 5'1 - 6'3. **Minimum age:** 20. **Language(s) preferred:** Bilingual an asset. F/A's receive an additional $1.50 hr. language pay.

SALARY AND EXPENSES: **Base pay/ hours minimum:** $1300. (50). **Overtime rate:** $23.32. **Per diem:** $1.65 Domestic $1.75 International **B-Scale:** None. **Uniform costs:** $600. **Training length/ location:** 5 weeks/ ATL. **Training cost:** None. **Salary earned while in training:** $805. **Company paid housing provided?** Yes. **Domiciles:** ATL ORD WAS BOS SLC LAX MCO MIA/FLL NYC SEA PDX MSY IAH DFW CVG. **Flight Attendant Union:** None.

APPLICATION ADDRESS: Delta Air Lines, Attn: Personnel Dept - Flight Attendant Hiring, P.O.Box 20530, Atlanta, GA 30320.

✈ EVERGREEN

Airline type: Charter.
Resume required? Yes, before submitting for an application.
SASE required with application? No. **Application retained:** 12 months. **Fee for applying:** None. **How many interviews/ what type?** Two- group/private. **Transportation to interview paid by airline?** No.

REQUIREMENTS: **Height:** 5'2 min. No maximum. **Minimum age:** 20. **Language(s) preferred:** Additional languages helpful.

SALARY AND EXPENSES: **Base pay/ hours minimum:** $1200. (65). **Overtime rate:** $18.50. **Per diem:** $30 Domestic - $48 Internat'l **B-Scale:** None. **Uniform costs:** None. **Training length/ location:** 3 weeks/ PDX/TUC. **Training cost:** None. **Salary earned while in training:** Yes. **Housing provided?** Yes. **Domiciles:** None. **Flight Attendant Union:** None.

APPLICATION ADDRESS: Evergreen Airlines, Attn: Shirley Martin, 3850 Three Mile Lane, McMinneville, OR 97128.

✈ EXECUTIVE AIR/AMEAGLE

Airline type: Scheduled.
Resume required? No. **SASE required with application?** Yes. **Application retained:** 24 months. **Fee for applying:** None. **How many interviews/ what type?** Two- group/private. **Transportation to interview paid by airline?** Yes.

REQUIREMENTS: **Height:** 5' - 5'10. **Minimum age:** 19. **Language(s) preferred:** Spanish.

SALARY AND EXPENSES: **Base pay/ hours minimum:** $755. (70). **Overtime rate:** $12. **Per diem:** $.50 **B-Scale:** None. **Uniform costs:** $750-800 50/50. **Training length/ location:** 3 1/2 weeks/ DFW. **Training cost:** None. **Salary earned while in training:** None. **Company paid housing provided?** Yes. **Domiciles:** SJU. **Flight Attendant Union:** Transport Workers Union.

APPLICATION ADDRESS: AMR Eagle Recruitment, MD 4121, P.O.Box 619415, DFW Airport, TX 75261-9415.

✈ EXPRESS ONE INTERNATIONAL AIRLINES

Airline type: Scheduled.

Resume required? Yes with picture. **SASE required with application?** Yes. **Application retained:** 12 months. **Fee for applying:** None. **How many interviews/ what type?** Two-group/private. Drop-in possible. **Transportation to interview paid by airline?** Yes.

REQUIREMENTS: **Height:** 5'2 - 6'. **Minimum age:** 21. **Language(s) preferred:** Spanish, German.

SALARY AND EXPENSES: **Base pay/ hours minimum:** $1200. (65). **Overtime rate:** $21.50. **Per diem:** $30 per day **B-Scale:** None. **Uniform costs:** $450. **Training length/ location:** 14-16 days DAL. **Training cost:** None. **Salary earned while in training:** $50 per day. **Company paid housing provided?** Yes. **Domiciles:** DAL ACY. **Flight Attendant Union:** None.

APPLICATION ADDRESS: Express One International Airlines, Attn: Flight Attendant Recruitment, 3890 West Northwest Hwy, Dallas, TX 75220.

✈ FAMILY AIRLINES

Airline type: Scheduled.

Resume required? Yes. **SASE required with application?** Yes. **Application retained:** 6 months. **Fee for applying:** None. **How many interviews/ what type?** Two- group/private. **Transportation to interview paid by airline?** No.

REQUIREMENTS: **Height:** None. **Minimum age:** 18. **Language(s) preferred:** None.

SALARY AND EXPENSES: **Base pay/ hours minimum:** $1100. (70). **Overtime rate:** None. **Per diem:** Not yet determined **B-Scale:** None. **Uniform costs:** Included. **Training length/ location:** 2 weeks/MSP. **Training cost:** $1950. **Salary earned while in training:** $24 per day. **Company paid housing provided?** Yes, and transportation. **Domiciles:** LAS. **Flight Attendant Union:** None.

APPLICATION ADDRESS: Family Airlines, 3035 E. Patrick Lane, Las Vegas, NV 89120.

✈ FLAGSHIP/AMEAGLE

Airline type: Scheduled.
Resume required? No. **SASE required with application?** Yes. **Application retained:** 24 months. **Fee for applying:** None. **How many interviews/ what type?** Two- group/one-on-one. **Transportation to interview paid by airline?** Yes.

REQUIREMENTS: **Height:** 5' - 5'10. **Minimum age:** 19. **Language(s) preferred:** None.

SALARY AND EXPENSES: **Base pay/ hours minimum:** $752.50 (70). **Overtime rate:** $10.75. **Per diem:** $1.00 **B-Scale:** None. **Uniform costs:** $750-$800 (50/50). **Training length/ location:** 3 1/2 weeks/DFW. **Training cost:** None. **Salary earned while in training:** None. **Company paid housing provided?** Yes. **Domiciles:** MIA JFK BNA RDU. **Flight Attendant Union:** None.

APPLICATION ADDRESS: AMR Eagle Flight Attendant Employment, P.O.Box 619415, Mail Drop 4121, DFW Airport, Ft.Worth, TX 75261-9415.

✈ HAWAIIAN

Airline type: Scheduled.
Resume required? Yes. **SASE required with application?** Yes. **Application retained:** 12 months. **Fee for applying:** None. **How many interviews/ what type?** Four to five various. **Transportation to interview paid by airline?** Yes.

REQUIREMENTS: **Height:** 5'2 - 6'. **Minimum age:** 20. **Language(s) preferred:** Japanese, French, Tongan, Samoan, Tahitian.

SALARY AND EXPENSES: **Base pay/ hours minimum:** $11.39 (75). **Overtime rate:** $11.39. **Per diem:** $1.80 Int'l. - $1.40 Inter-island **B-Scale:** None. **Uniform costs:** $450. **Training length/ location:** 6 weeks/ HNL. **Training cost:** None. **Salary earned while in training:** $4.35 hr. **Company paid housing provided?** No. **Domiciles:** PHL LAX HNL. **Flight Attendant Union:** Association of Flight Attendants.

APPLICATION ADDRESS: Hawaiian Airlines, Attn: Flight Attendant Recruitment, P.O.Box 30008, Honolulu, HI 96820.

✈ HORIZION AIR

Airline type: Scheduled.

Resume required? Yes. **SASE required with application?** Yes. **Application retained:** 6 months. **Fee for applying:** None. **How many interviews/ what type?** Three- group/role play/private. **Transportation to interview paid by airline?** Yes.

REQUIREMENTS: **Height:** Proportional. **Minimum age:** 21. **Language(s) preferred:** None.

SALARY AND EXPENSES: **Base pay/ hours minimum:** $925. **Overtime rate:** None. **Per diem:** $1.05 **B-Scale:** None. **Uniform costs:** $500. **Training length/ location:** 3 weeks/ PDX. **Training cost:** None. **Salary earned while in training:.** Per diem. **Company paid housing provided?** Yes, out of town candidates only. **Domiciles:** PDX BOI. **Flight Attendant Union:** Association of Flight Attendants.

APPLICATION ADDRESS: Horizion Air, Attn: Personnel Department, P.O.Box 48309, Seattle, WA 98148.

✈ JETSTREAM INTERNATIONAL

Airline type: Charter.

Resume required? Yes. **SASE required with application?** No. **Application retained:** 6 months. **Fee for applying:** None. **How many interviews/ what type?** Two - group/individual. **Transportation to interview paid by airline?** On-line.

REQUIREMENTS: **Height:** No minimum - 5'7. **Minimum age:** 21. **Language(s) preferred:** French.

SALARY AND EXPENSES: **Base pay/ hours minimum:** $12.75 (70). **Overtime rate:** None. **Per diem:** $1.00 **B-Scale:** None. **Uniform costs:** $500-$1000. **Training length/ location:** 3 weeks/DAY. **Training cost:** None. **Salary earned while in training:** $160 per week, plus per diem. **Company paid housing provided?** Yes. **Domiciles:** IND PIT. **Flight Attendant Union:** None.

APPLICATION ADDRESS: Jetstream International, 3401 Park Center Drive Suite 290, Dayton, OH 45414.

✈ KEY AIR

Airline type: Scheduled.

Resume required? Yes, before applying. **SASE required with application?** Yes. **Application retained:** 12 months. **Fee for applying:** None. **How many interviews/ what type?** 1 - 2 private. **Transportation to interview paid by airline?** No.

REQUIREMENTS: **Height:** None. **Minimum age:** 21. **Language(s) preferred:** Second language a plus.

SALARY AND EXPENSES: **Base pay/ hours minimum:** $950. (65). **Overtime rate:** $15. hr. **Per diem:** $1.10 per hour for overnite **B-Scale:** None. **Uniform costs:** $90-$250. **Training length/ location:** 3 weeks/-SAV. **Training cost:** None. **Salary earned while in training:** None. **Company paid housing provided?** No. **Domiciles:** SAV. **Flight Attendant Union:** International Brotherhood of Teamsters.

APPLICATION ADDRESS: Key Air Inc., Attn: Jack Bridges, P.O.Box 7709, Savannah Airport , GA 31418-7709.

✈ MARK AIR

Airline type: Scheduled.

Resume required? Yes. **SASE required with application?** Yes. **Application retained:** 3 months. **Fee for applying:** None. **How many interviews/ what type?** Two - group/individual. **Transportation to interview paid by airline?** No.

REQUIREMENTS: **Height:** 5'1 - no maximum. **Minimum age:** 21. **Language(s) preferred:** None.

SALARY AND EXPENSES: **Base pay/ hours minimum:** $9.20 (40). **Overtime rate:** $14.70. **Per diem:** $25 overnite only **B-Scale:** None. **Uniform costs:** $250 (50/50). **Training length/ location:** 3 weeks/ ANK or SEA. **Training cost:** None. **Salary earned while in training:** None. **Company paid housing provided?** No. **Domiciles:** ANK/SEA. **Flight Attendant Union:** None.

APPLICATION ADDRESS: Mark Air, Attn: Human Resources., P.O.Box 196769, Anchorage, AK 99519.

✈ MGM

Airline type: Charter.

Resume required? Yes. **SASE required with application?** No. **Application retained:** 6 months. **Fee for applying: None.** **How many interviews/ what type?** 3- Group/private/private. **Transportation to interview paid by airline?** No.

REQUIREMENTS: **Height:** 5'2. **Minimum age:** 21. **Language(s) preferred:** Japanese, Spanish.

SALARY AND EXPENSES: **Base pay/ hours minimum:** $16.61 (66). **Overtime rate:** 79-89 hours @ $8.00; 90+ hours @ $12.00. **Per diem:** Dom. - $1.40 Int'l. $2.00 **B-Scale:** None. **Uniform costs:** Paid by MGM. **Training length/ location:** 4 weeks/ LAX. **Training cost:** None. **Salary earned while in training:** $750 per month. **Company paid housing provided?** None. **Domiciles:** LAX. **Flight Attendant Union:** None.

APPLICATION ADDRESS: MGM Grand Air, Attn: Human Resourses, 1500 Rosecrans Suite 350, Manhatten Beach, CA 90254.

✈ MIAMI AIR

Airline type: Charter.

Resume required? Yes, plus photo. **SASE required with application?** No. **Application retained:** Until next open house. **Fee for applying:** None. **How many interviews/what type?** Two - group/personal. **Transportation to interview paid by airline?** No.

REQUIREMENTS: **Height:** 5'2 minimum. **Min. age:** 21. **Language(s) preferred:** Spanish & other European languages.

SALARY AND EXPENSES: **Base pay/ hours minimum:** $13. (70). **Overtime rate:** $13. **Per diem:** $1.25 **B-Scale:** None. **Uniform costs:** $800. **Training length/ location:** 3.5 weeks/ MIA **Training cost:** None. **Salary earned while in training:** $100.00 per week. **Company paid housing provided?** No. **Domiciles:** MIA. **Flight Attendant Union:** None.

APPLICATION ADDRESS: Miami Air, Attn: In-flight Recruitment, 815 NW 57th Ave. Suite 130, Miami, FL 33126.

✈ MIDWEST EXPRESS

Airline type: Scheduled.

Resume required? No. **SASE required with application?** No. **Application retained:** 12 months. **Fee for applying:** None. **How many interviews/ what type?** 3 - private. **Transportation to interview paid by airline?** On-line.

REQUIREMENTS: **Height:** 5'2 minimum. **Minimum age:** 20. **Language(s) preferred:** None.

SALARY AND EXPENSES: **Base pay/ hours minimum:** $14,800. **Overtime rate:** Time and a half. **Per diem:** $1.00; $1.30 for overnite. **B-Scale:** None. **Uniform costs:** $400. **Training length/ location:** 6 weeks/ MKE. **Training cost:** None. **Salary earned while in training:** Full salary. **Company paid housing provided?** No. **Domiciles:** MKE. **Flight Attendant Union:** None.

APPLICATION ADDRESS: Midwest Express, Mitchell International Airport, 4915 S. Howell, Milwaukee, WI 53207.

✈ NORTH AMERICAN

Airline type: Charter.

Resume required? No. **SASE required with application?** No. **Application retained:** 6 months. **Fee for applying:** None. **How many interviews/ what type?** Two - group/private. **Transportation to interview paid by airline?** No.

REQUIREMENTS: **Height:** 5'1 - 6'2. **Minimum age:** 18. **Language(s) preferred:** Hebrew, Spanish, French.

SALARY AND EXPENSES: **Base pay/ hours minimum:** $18.00 (67). **Overtime rate:** 120%. **Per diem:** $1.60 **B-Scale:** None. **Uniform costs:** $600. **Training length/ location:** 4 weeks/ JFK. **Training cost:** None. **Salary earned while in training:** $25 per day. **Company paid housing provided?** Partial. **Domiciles:** JFK. **Flight Attendant Union:** None.

APPLICATION ADDRESS: North American Airlines, JFK International Airport, Building 75, North Hanger Road, Jamaica NY 11430.

✈ NORTHWEST AIRLINES

Airline type: Scheduled.
Resume required? No. **SASE req'd with application?** Preferred. **Application retained:** 6 months. **Fee for applying:** None. **How many interviews/ type?** Two - group;group/private. **Transportation to interview paid by airline?** Yes.

REQUIREMENTS: **Height:** 5'0 min. No maximum. **Minimum age:** 19. **Language(s) preferred:** Japanese, Cantonese/Mandarin, or Korean required.

SALARY AND EXPENSES: **Base pay/ hours minimum:** $1008. (65). **Overtime rate:** $15.51 **Per diem:** $1.60 Dom. $1.80 Int'l. **B-Scale:** 6 years. **Uniform costs:** $600-$800. **Training length/ location:** 6 weeks/ MSP. **Training cost:** None. **Salary earned while in training:** Per diem. **Company paid housing provided?** Yes. **Domiciles:** MSP DTW HNL MEM SFO LAX SEA ORD BOS NYC. **Flight Attendant Union:** International Brotherhood of Teamsters.

APPLICATION ADDRESS: Northwest Airlines, Attn: Human Resources, Mail Stop F5480, 5101 Northwest Dr. Dept. A1410, St.Paul, MN 55111-3034.

✈ NORTHWEST AIRLINK EXPRESS ONE

Airline type: Scheduled.
Resume req'd? No. **SASE req'd with application?** Yes, with resume. **Application retained:** 6 months. **Fee for applying:** Unsolicited resumes: $10. **How many interviews/ what type?** Three - group/panel/private. **Transport'n to interview paid by airline?** $30 Service charge pass for 1st interview, follow-up is free.

REQUIREMENTS: **Height:** 5'1 - 5'9. **Minimum age:** 19. **Language(s) preferred:** None.

SALARY AND EXPENSES: **Base pay/ hours minimum:** $910. mo. MEM/MSP, $835. others. **Overtime rate:** None. **Per diem:** $14.00 overnite **B-Scale:** None. **Uniform costs:** $400. **Training length/ location:** 2 1/2 weeks/ MEM. **Training cost:** None. **Salary earned while in training:** $15.00 per day. **Company paid housing provided?** Yes. **Domiciles:** MEM GPT PNS MSP plus satallites. **Flight Attendant Union:** None.

APPLICATION ADDRESS: Northwest Airlink/ Express One, 1777 Phoenix Parkway Suite 303, Atlanta, GA 30349.

✈ PARADISE ISLAND AIR

Airline type: Scheduled.

Resume required? No. **SASE required with application?** No. **Application retained:** 6 months. **Fee for applying:** None. **How many interviews/ what type?** Two - group/private. **Transportation to interview paid by airline?** No.

REQUIREMENTS: **Height:** 5'3 minimum. **Minimum age:** 21. **Language(s) preferred:** None.

SALARY AND EXPENSES: **Base pay/ hours minimum:** $53 per day (85). **Overtime rate:** $18. **Per diem:** $3 per day; $40 island overnite **B-Scale:** None. **Uniform costs:** $130. **Training length/ location:** 2 weeks/ FLL. **Training cost:** None. **Salary earned while in training:** $53. per day. **Company paid housing provided?** No. **Domiciles:** FLL. **Flight Attendant Union:** None.

APPLICATION ADDRESS: Paradise Island Airlines, Attn: IFS Manager, P.O.Box 350510, Ft.Lauderdale, FL 33335.

✈ REEVE ALEUTIAN AIRWAYS

Airline type: Scheduled.

Resume required? No. **SASE required with application?** No. **Application retained:** 12 months. **Fee for applying:** None. **How many interviews/ what type?** Two - group/private. **Transportation to interview paid by airline?** Yes, on-line.

REQUIREMENTS: **Height:** 5'2 minimum. **Minimum age:** 21. **Language(s) preferred:** None.

SALARY AND EXPENSES: **Base pay/ hours minimum:** $1300. (66). **Overtime rate:** $15. **Per diem:** None. **B-Scale:** None. **Uniform costs:** $400. **Training length/ location:** 4 weeks/ ANK. **Training cost:** None. **Salary earned while in training:** $20 per day. **Company paid housing provided?** No. **Domiciles:** ANK. **Flight Attendant Union:** None.

APPLICATION ADDRESS: Reeve Aleutian Airways, Attn: Director In-Flight Services, 4700 W. Internatioal Airport Road, Anchorage, AK 99502.

✈ RENO AIR

Airline type: Scheduled.

Resume required? Preferred. **SASE required with application?** Yes. **Application retained:** 6 months. **Fee for applying:** None. **How many interviews/ what type?** Two - group/two-on-two. **Transportation to interview paid by airline?** Yes, on-line.

REQUIREMENTS: **Height:** 5'1. **Minimum age:** 21. **Language(s) preferred:** None.

SALARY AND EXPENSES: **Base pay/ hours minimum:** $13. (70). **Overtime rate:** $13. **Per diem:** $24 per overnite **B-Scale:** None. **Uniform costs:** $300. **Training length/ location:** 4 weeks/ RNO. **Training cost:** None. **Salary earned while in training:** $35 per diem. **Company paid housing provided?** No. **Domiciles:** RNO SJC. **Flight Attendant Union:** None.

APPLICATION ADDRESS: Reno Air, Attn: Director Human Resources, 690 Plum Lane, Reno NV 89502.

✈ RICH INTERNATIONAL

Airline type: Charter.

Resume required? No. **SASE required with application?** Yes. **Application retained:** 12 months. **Fee for applying:** None. **How many interviews/ what type?** Two - group/private. **Transport'n to interview paid by airline?** No.

REQUIREMENTS: **Height:** 5'2 - 6'. **Minimum age:** 21. **Language(s) preferred:** Portuguese, French, German, Spanish, Italian.

SALARY AND EXPENSES: **Base pay/ hours minimum:** $12.50 hr. **Overtime rate:** $12.50 hr. **Per diem:** $1.25 Dom. $1.50 Int'l. $2.00 Italy **B-Scale:** None. **Uniform costs:** $250. **Training length/ location:** 2 weeks/MIA. **Training cost:** None. **Salary earned while in training:** None. **Company paid housing provided?** No. **Domiciles:** MIA. **Flight Attendant Union:** None.

APPLICATION ADDRESS: Rich International, Attn: In-Flight, P.O.Box 522067, Miami, FL 33152.

✈ SKYWEST AIRLINES DELTA CONNECTION

Airline type: Scheduled.

Resume required? No. **SASE required with application?** Yes. **Application retained:** 6 months. **Fee for applying:** $15. **How many interviews/ what type?** 3 - Group/individual/individual. **Transportion to interview paid by airline?** No.

REQUIREMENTS: **Height:** 5'8 maximum. **Minimum age:** 21. **Language(s) preferred:** None.

SALARY AND EXPENSES: **Base pay/ hours minimum:** $975. (75). **Overtime rate:** $13. **Per diem:** $1.20 **B-Scale:** None. **Uniform costs:** $300. **Training length/ location:** 18 days /SLC. **Training cost:** None. **Salary earned while in training:** $480. after 30 days on-line. **Company paid housing provided?** No. **Domiciles:** PSP SLC SAN MRY. **Flight Attendant Union:** None.

APPLICATION ADDRESS: Skywest Airlines, 444 S. River Road, St. George, UT 84122.

✈ SOUTHWEST AIRLINES

Airline type: Scheduled.

Resume required? No. **SASE required with application?** No. **Application retained:** 6 months. **Fee for applying:** $20. **How many interviews/ what type?** Four- group/private/private/private. **Transportation to interview paid by airline?** On-line only.

REQUIREMENTS: **Height:** 75 inch reach. **Minimum age:** 20. **Language(s) preferred:** Spanish.

SALARY AND EXPENSES: **Base pay/ hours minimum:** $13.60 per trip (/Trip= 243 flight miles). **Overtime rate:** None. **Per diem:** $2. **B-Scale:** None. **Uniform costs:** $600. **Training length/ location:** 5 weeks/ SWA HQ. **Training cost:** None. **Salary earned while in training:** None. **Company paid housing provided?** Non-Dallas residents. **Domiciles:** DAL PHX HOU. **Flight Attendant Union:** Transport Workers Union.

APPLICATION ADDRESS: Southwestern Airlines, P.O.Box 36611, Love Field, Dallas, TX 75235.

✈ SUN COUNTRY

Airline type: Charter.

Resume required? Yes, resumes only. **SASE required with application?** Yes. **Application retained:** 12 months. **Fee for applying:** None. **How many interviews/ type?** Two - group/private. **Transportation to interview paid by airline?** On-line.

REQUIREMENTS: **Height:** None. **Minimum age:** None. **Language(s) preferred:** None.

SALARY AND EXPENSES: **Base pay/ hours minimum:** $16.00 (60). **Overtime rate:** None. **Per diem:** $1.25 Domestic. $1.50 International **B-Scale:** None. **Uniform costs:** $550. **Training length/ location:** 4 weeks/MSP. **Training cost:** None. **Salary earned while in training:** $40 per day. **Company paid housing provided?** No. **Domiciles:** MSP. **Flight Attendant Union:** None.

APPLICATION ADDRESS: Sun Country Airlines, Attn: Human Resources, 7701 26th Ave. So., Minneapolis, MN 55450.

✈ TOWER AIR

Airline type: Charter.

Resume required? Preferred. **SASE required with application?** No. **Application retained:** 12 months. **Fee for applying:** None. **How many interviews/ what type?** Three-group/group/private. **Transportation to interview paid by airline?** No.

REQUIREMENTS: **Height:** None. **Minimum age:** 18. **Language(s) preferred:** French, Scandinavian, German, Spanish, Portuguese, Italian, Greek.

SALARY AND EXPENSES: **Base pay/ hours minimum:** $13 (55). **Overtime rate:** $2-$7.50 depending on hours worked. **Per diem:** $1.90 Int'l. $1.50 Dom. **B-Scale:** None. **Uniform costs:** $750. **Training length/ location:** 3 weeks/JFK. **Training cost:** $150. **Salary earned while in training:** None. **Company paid housing provided?** No. **Domiciles:** JFK MIA. **Flight Attendant Union:** Association of Flight Attendants.

APPLICATION ADDRESS: Tower Air, Attn: In-Flight Services - Flight Attendant Hiring, JFK Int'l. Airport, Hanger 8, Jamacia, NY 11430.

✈ ULTRAIR

Airline type: Scheduled.

Resume required? Yes. **SASE required with application?** Yes. **Application retained:** 6 months. **Fee for applying:** None. **How many interviews/ what type?** Three-group/group/personal. **Transportation to interview paid by airline?** No.

REQUIREMENTS: **Height:** 5'2 -6'2. **Minimum age:** 20. **Language(s) preferred:** None.

SALARY AND EXPENSES: **Base pay/ hours minimum:** $1200. (60). **Overtime rate:** $20. **Per diem:** $1.25. **B-Scale:** None. **Uniform costs:** $600. **Training length/ location:** 3 weeks/ Varies. **Training cost:** None. **Salary earned while in training:** None. **Company paid housing provided?** Undetermined. **Domiciles:** HOU (must live in Houston). **Flight Attendant Union:** None.

APPLICATION ADDRESS: Ultra Air, Attn: Roderic Quinn, 3100 N. Terminal Road, P.O.Box 60052, Houston, TX 77205.

✈ UNITED AIRLINES

Airline type: Scheduled.

Resume required? No. **SASE required with application?** No. **Application retained:** 12 months. **Fee for applying:** $20. **How many interviews/ what type?** Two- group, group/private. **Transportation to interview paid by airline?** Yes.

REQUIREMENTS: **Height:** 5'2 -6'. **Minimum age:** 19. **Language(s) preferred:** Cantonese, Mandarin, Japanese, French, Spanish, Korean, German, Italian, Portuguese.

SALARY AND EXPENSES: **Base pay/ hours minimum:** $1,101 (65). **Overtime rate:** $16.94. **Per diem:** $1.65. **B-Scale:** None. **Uniform costs:** $700. **Training length/ location:** 7 weeks/ ORD. **Training cost:** None. **Salary earned while in training:** None. **Company paid housing provided?** Yes. **Domiciles:** DEN NYC EWR ORD DCA TPE LAX SFO SEA HNL LHR CDG. **Flight Attendant Union:** Association of Flight Attendants.

APPLICATION ADDRESS: United Airlines, Application Request Center, EXOES P.O.Box 66100, Chicago, IL 60666.

✈ USAIR

Airline type: Scheduled.
Resume required? No. **SASE required with application?**
Yes. **Application retained:** 6 months. **Fee for applying:** $10.
How many interviews/ what type? Three- group/private/private. **Transportation to interview paid by airline?** Yes, space available.

REQUIREMENTS: **Height:** No requirements. **Minimum age:** 21. **Language(s) preferred:** French, German & Spanish.

SALARY AND EXPENSES: **Base pay/ hours minimum:** $14.61 (65). **Overtime rate:** None. **Per diem:** $1.65 **B-Scale:** 5 years. **Uniform costs:** $1,000. **Training length/ location:** 5 weeks/ PIT & CLT. **Training cost:** None. **Salary earned while in training:** $125 per week. **Company paid housing provided?** Yes. **Domiciles:** BAL BOS CLT PHL PIT SFO LAX DCA. **Flight Attendant Union:** Association of Flight Attendants.

APPLICATION ADDRESS: USAir, Employment Services Dept., Washington National Airport, Washington, DC 20001.

✈ USAIR
HENSEN AVIATION

Airline type: Scheduled.
Resume required? Yes. **SASE required with application?**
Yes. **Application retained:** 6 months. **Fee for applying:** None.
How many interviews/ what type? Henson interview process.
Transportation to interview paid by airline? On-line.

REQUIREMENTS: **Height:** No height requirement. **Minimum age:** 21. **Language(s) preferred:** None.

SALARY AND EXPENSES: **Base pay/ hours minimum:** $13.50 (70). **Overtime rate:** $13.50 **Per diem:** $1.10 **B-Scale:** None. **Uniform costs:** $350 - 400. **Training length/ location:** 2 1/2 weeks/SBY. **Training cost:** None. **Salary earned while in training:** Monthly guarantee pro-rated daily. **Company paid housing provided?** Yes. **Domiciles:** SBY LYH ORF/PHF EWN JAX. **Flight Attendant Union:** Association of Flight Attendants.

APPLICATION ADDRESS: Hensen Aviation, Attn: Personnel, Salsbury/Wicomico Airport, Salsbury, MD 21801.

✈ USAIR SHUTTLE

Airline type: Scheduled.

Resume required? Yes. **SASE required with application?** No. **Application retained:** 12 months. **Fee for applying:** None. **How many interviews/ what type?** Three- group/group/private. **Transportation to interview paid by airline?** No.

REQUIREMENTS: **Height:** 5'- 6'. **Minimum age:** 18. **Language(s) preferred:** None.

SALARY AND EXPENSES: **Base pay/ hours minimum:** $817 (67). **Overtime rate:** $12.20 **Per diem:** None. **B-Scale:** Yes. **Uniform costs:** None. **Training length/ location:** 2 weeks/ BOS. **Training cost:** None. **Salary earned while in training:** None. **Company paid housing provided?** Yes. **Domiciles:** BOS NYC DCA. **Flight Attendant Union:** Transport Workers Union.

APPLICATION ADDRESS: USAir Shuttle, P.O.Box 616, LaGuardia Airport, Flushing, NY 11371.

✈ WESTAIR

Airline type: Scheduled.

Resume required? Yes. **SASE required with application?** Yes. **Application retained:** 12 months. **Fee for applying:** None. **How many interviews/ what type?** Two- group/private. **Transportation to interview paid by airline?** On-line.

REQUIREMENTS: **Height:** 4'11 - 5'8. **Minimum age:** 21. **Language(s) preferred:** None.

SALARY AND EXPENSES: **Base pay/ hours minimum:** $11.75 (75). **Overtime rate:** $11.75. **Per diem:** $.95 **B-Scale:**. **Uniform costs:** $600. **Training length/ location:** 4 weeks/ FAT. **Training cost:** None. **Salary earned while in training:** $4 hr. **Company paid housing provided?** No. **Domiciles:** SFO FAT SEA LAX SAC. **Flight Attendant Union:** Association of Flight Attendants.

APPLICATION ADDRESS: Westair, Attn. Flight Attendant Employment, 5570 Air Terminal Drive, Fresno, CA 93727.

✈ WINGS WEST/AMEAGLE

Airline type: Scheduled.

Resume required? No. **SASE required with application?** Yes. **Application retained:** 24 months. **Fee for applying:** None. **How many interviews/ what type?** Two- group/one-on-one. **Transportation to interview paid by airline?** Yes.

REQUIREMENTS: **Height:** 5' - 5'10. **Minimum age:** 19. **Language(s) preferred:** None.

SALARY AND EXPENSES: **Base pay/ hours minimum:** $752.50 (70). **Overtime rate:** $10.75. **Per diem:** $1.00. **B-Scale:** None. **Uniform costs:** None. **Training length/ location:** 3 1/2 weeks/DFW. **Training cost:** None. **Salary earned while in training:** None. **Company paid housing provided?** Yes. **Domiciles:** LAX SJC. **Flight Attendant Union:** Transport Workers Union.

APPLICATION ADDRESS: AMR Eagle Recruitment, MD 4121, P.O.Box 619415, DFW Airport, TX 75261-9415.

✈ WORLD AIRWAYS

Airline type: Charter.

Resume required? Yes, resumes only. **SASE required with application?** No. **Application retained:** 6 months. **Fee for applying:** None. **How many interviews/ what type?** Varies. **Transportation to interview paid by airline?** No.

REQUIREMENTS: **Height:** Proportional. **Minimum age:** 21. **Language(s) preferred:** Second language a plus.

SALARY AND EXPENSES: **Base pay/ hours minimum:** $1050. (65). **Overtime rate:** Not given. **Per diem:** $1.55. **B-Scale:** None. **Uniform costs:** $700. **Training length/ location:** 4 weeks/PHL. **Training cost:** None. **Salary earned while in training:** None. **Company paid housing provided?** No. **Domiciles:** PHL CHS. **Flight Attendant Union:** International Brotherhood of Teamsters.

APPLICATION ADDRESS: World Airways, Attn: Human Resources, 13873 Park Center Rd Suite 490, Herndon, VA 22071.

✈ INFORMATION UPDATES

The information contained herein changes much too quickly to remain current for the duration of this guide. To receive information updates, changes in the airline listings, additions and deletions of airlines, simply send a stamped self-addressed envelope to:

Flight Attendant Career Guide
Information Updates
P.O.Box 6455
Delray Beach, FL 33484-6455

The information will be sent to you in the next day's mail.

✈ ABOUT THE AUTHOR

TIM KIRKWOOD was born in Bloomington, Minnesota in 1953, and began his traveling career with a sales position that led him to the Southeastern U.S., and eventually, to California. He began his flying career in San Francisco in 1976, and has been based in Kansas City, Boston and New York City. He has survived deregulation, labor disputes, cut-backs, and corporate take-overs.

The flexible scheduling of his flight attendant career has afforded him the opportunity to pursue many other vocations, including disk jockey, tour director, bartender and author. He has also been involved in many volunteer activities for charity. The constant use of his travel benefits has given him the chance to excel as a professional photographer in both standard and stereo (3-D) formats. Tim currently resides in South Florida.

✈ SIGN YOUR FRIENDS UP!

Many of your friends may be interested in becoming flight attendants for today's airlines. Pass on this handy order form to them. After all, it's much more fun to work with friends!

YES! I want to receive a copy of the FLIGHT ATTENDANT CAREER GUIDE. I have enclosed my check or money order for $14.95, plus $2 shipping and handling for each copy. (Florida residents please add 6% state sales tax) *Please rush my copy to:*

Name:_____

Address:_____

City: _____ State:____ Zip:_____

**SEND
TO:** Flight Attendant Career Guide
P.O.Box 6455
Delray Beach, FL 33484-6455

Thomas Jefferson's Cook Book

By
MARIE KIMBALL

*Th: Jefferson
presents his compliments to*

*and requests the favour of his company
to dinner on   next
at half after three o'clock.*

The favour of an answer is requested.

MCMXXXVIII
RICHMOND • GARRETT&MASSIE • PUBLISHERS

Published by:

James Direct, Inc.

500 S. Prospect Ave.

Hartville, Ohio 44632

U.S.A.

This historic edition produced by
Murry Broach Productions

Originally printed in 1938 by:
GARRETT AND MASSIE, INCORPORATED
RICHMOND, VIRGINIA
Part of the material in the text, which appeared in an article by the writer
in the *Virginia Quarterly Review*, is included by its kind permission.

ISBN: 1-883944-33-3

Printing 12 11 10 9 8 7 6 5 4 3 2 1

MANUFACTURED IN THE UNITED STATES OF AMERICA

Fourth Edition   Copyright 2007   James Direct, Inc.

CONTENTS

	PAGE
THE EPICURE OF MONTICELLO	1
JEFFERSON'S PARIS RECIPES	27
THE MONTICELLO RECIPES	33
SOUPS	35
MEATS AND FOWL	45
FISH	68
VEGETABLES	73
PUDDINGS	77
CREAMS	98
FRENCH RECEIPTS	111

THOMAS JEFFERSON'S COOK BOOK

THE EPICURE OF MONTICELLO

"The whole of my life has been a war with my natural tastes, feelings and wishes," Thomas Jefferson remarked in wistful retrospect on his retirement from the presidency. "Domestic life and literary pursuits were my first and my latest inclinations, circumstances and not my desires led me to the path I have trod." It is not surprising, in view of this confession, to find that our first Democratic President, whom we tend to think of as occupied with such lofty thoughts and ideas as are embodied in the Declaration of Independence or the Statute of Virginia for Religious Freedom, was one of the greatest epicures and connoisseurs of the art of living, of his day. The choicest delicacies of two continents made their appearance on the presidential table, the finest wines were imported from France and Italy, the food was prepared by French chefs, and the whole was supervised by the President himself.

Jefferson had been left a widower early in life and the management of his household, as well as his plantations, fell upon him. He showed the same interest and punctiliousness in his domestic affairs as he did in those of state. The selection of a cook or a maître d'hôtel was given no less thought than the choice of a minister plenipotentiary. He penned a rule for "Nouilly à macaroni" with the gravity that he signed a treaty. It was no unusual thing for him to pause in his official duties to write his daughter: "I enclose you Lemaire's receipts. The orthography will be puzzling and amusing but the receipts are valuable." The receipt was for "pannequaiques."

When Jefferson set sail for France in 1785, as

Minister Plenipotentiary to the court of Louis XVI, he was, all unwittingly, leaving behind him the Virginia tradition of ham, fried chicken, Brunswick stew, greens and batter bread. The cuisine of France was a joy and a revelation to him. During the four years he lived in Paris Jefferson devoted himself to the intricacies of French cooking. The most precious recipes of the cuisinière, whom he employed at three hundred francs a year, with an allowance of one hundred francs for wine, were carefully copied in his own hand and brought back to the United States. Thus it happens that our first American recipe for ice cream, then no vulgar commonplace, is in the writing of a President of the United States.

Although General Washington seems to have had the first ice cream freezer on record-he noted that in May, 1784, he spent "1. 13. 4 By a cream machine for Ice"-Martha Washington's numerous recipes do not include one for ice cream. Jefferson, however, made his as follows:

2 bottles of good cream

6 yolks of eggs

1/2 lb. of sugar

mix the yolks and sugar

put the cream on a fire in a casserole first putting in a stick of vanilla

When near boiling take it off and pour it gently into the mixture of eggs and sugar

Stir it well.

put it on the fire again stirring it thoroughly with a spoon to prevent its sticking to the casserole.

When near boiling take it off and strain it through a towel.

put it in the sorbetière (ice pail).
then set it in ice an hour before it is to be served.
Put into the ice a handful of salt
put ice all around the sorbetière
i.e. a layer of ice a layer of salt for 3 layers.
put salt on the coverlid of the sorbetière & cover the whole with ice
leave it still half a quarter of an hour
Then turn the S. in the ice 10 min.
Open it to loosen with a spatula the ice from the inner sides of the S.
Open it from time to time to detach the ice from the sides
When well taken (prise) stir it well with the spatula
put it in moulds, jostling it well down on the knee
then put the mould into the same bucket of ice
leave it there to the moment of serving it.
to withdraw it, immerse the mould in warm water, tossing it well until it will come out & turn it into a plate.

This ice cream was served in a more elaborate way on state occasions in a manner somewhat similar to the "Baked Alaska" so favored during the opulent nineties. One visitor to the White House reports that at a presidential dinner the ice cream was brought to the table in the form of small balls, enclosed in cases of warm pastry, a feat that caused great astonishment and murmurings. Indeed, Jefferson's predeliction for intricate dishes, usually of French origin, was at times the occasion for unfavorable comment, no matter how palatable they had proven to his guests. His great antagonist, Patrick Henry, denounced him, in a political speech, as a man who had "abjured his native victuals," and was unfaithful to good, old-fashioned roast beef.

An ice was but one of the delicacies Jefferson learned to make in France. His servants were interviewed and his friends implored to yield the secrets of the kitchen. "Biscuits de Savoye, Blanc Manger, Meringues, Macarons and Quacking Jellies" were favored eighteenth-century viands for which Jefferson diligently transcribed the recipes. Sometimes they were in English, sometimes in French, now and then partly in each. The ingenious rule for "Wine Jellies" begins gaily in English: "take 4 calves feet & wash without taking off the hoofs. These feet must be well boiled the day before they are wanted." The "Meringues," however, are thoroughly "hyphenated:" "12 blanc d'oeuf, les fouettes bien fermes, 12 cueillèrres de sucre en poudre, put them by little and little into the whites of eggs, fouetter le tout ensemble, dresser les sur un papier avec un cueiller de bouche, metter les dans un four bien doux, that is to say an oven after the bread is drawn out. You may leave them there as long as you please."

After Jefferson's departure from France, in 1789, William Short, his protégé and confidential secretary, left in Paris as chargé d'affaires, was pressed into service, and it is not unusual to find among the diplomatic papers that were dispatched across the sea, detailed instructions "de faire cuire un poulet en cassette," or some other delicacy. Short even made a special trip to Naples to secure a "maccaroni mould" for Jefferson, in order that his patron might indulge in this favorite food. He writes: "It is of a smaller

diameter than that used at the manufactories of
maccaroni, but of the same diameter with others that
have been sent to gentlemen in other countries. I
went to see them made. I observed that the macaroni
most esteemed at Naples was smaller than that
generally seen at Paris. This is the part of Italy most
famous for the excellence of the article." Short was
unaware that among the macaroni-cognoscenti this
was known as spaghetti.

Lemaire, Jefferson's faithful maitre d'hôtel during
his presidency, contributed a disquisition on the use
of wines in cooking: "Facon Demployer differents sorte
de vin a Lusage de la cuisine francaise," probably our
earliest written record, in America, of this refinement
in the art of cooking. The author's orthographical
accomplishments were scarcely greater in French
than in English.

Boef a la mode . . . . 1/2 peinte de vin blanc
Veau a l'estaufade . . . . . . 1/2 idem de blanc
Dindon a la daube . . . . . . 1/2 idem . . idem.
Matelot de paicon . . . . . . 1/2 idem de rouge
Une fricassee de lupin . . . 1/2 idem de rouge
Un Gâteau au ri . . . . une peinte de sherry,
          pour la sauce mariné
Les Beg'nais de pomme . . 1/2 Goblet d'au vie
Les Beg'nais de pain . . . . 1/2 peinte de madeira
Poutain a l'anglaise . . . . . 1 peinte pour la sauce

From Petit, who entered his service in Paris as valet
de chambre and was subsequently promoted to the
rank of maître d'hôtel "in consequence of embezzle-
ments and depredations committed by M. Marc, the
late controller of Finances in his Department,"
Jefferson secured a recipe for making coffee which he

ever after used. The terse annotation concluding
the "rule" is but one of the many evidences of the
meticulous care with which the President watched
every detail of his household.

On one measure of the coffee ground into meal
pour three measures of boiling water, boil it, on hot
ashes mixed w. coal, till the meal disappears from
the top, when it will be precipitated. Pour it three
times through a flannel strainer, it will yield 2 1/3
measures of clear coffee. An ounce of coffee meal
makes 1 1/2 cups of clear coffee in this way. The
flannel must be rinced out in hot or cold water for
every making.

Tea was likewise subject to his careful scrutiny and
scientific observation, as well as sugar. He notes in
his account book:

Feb. 8.

Tea out. The pound has lasted exactly 7 weeks,
used 6 times a week. This is 8/21 or .4 of an oz. a
time, for a single person. A pound of tea making
126 cups costs 2 D. 126 cups or ounces of coffee =
8 lb. cost 1.6. Campbell, 1 lb. Imperial tea 2.

Feb. 18.

on trial it takes 11 dwt Troy of double refd maple
sugar to a dish of coffee or 1 lb avoirdupoise to 26.5
dishes, so that at 20 cents per lb. it is 8 mills per
dish. An ounce of coffee at 20 cents per lb. is 12.5
mills so that sugar & coffee for a dish is worth two
cents.

During the years he was president Jefferson found
time to keep a careful table of the earliest and latest
appearance of each vegetable on the Washington

market. No less than thirty-seven kinds are listed. It is noteworthy that such delicacies as mushrooms, broccoli, and endive, which have become a commonplace on the American market only in the last decade, were no strangers to the presidential table in 1800. Broccoli is listed as being in season from April seventh to twentieth, Mushrooms from the eleventh of August to the nineteenth of October-an odd season from our point of view, and endive from September twentyseventh to February twenty-ninth.

Not only was such a minute account kept of the seasonable vegetables in market, but, in his "Garden Book," Jefferson likewise noted the time each vegetable grown at Monticello was sown, its name and "pedigree," for he often imported seeds or got them from neighbors or friends, along with the time it came to table. Thus, in 1774, after minute and elaborate annotations as to the planting of his garden, and whether the seeds were from Italy, from England, from Tuckahoe, from Dr. Brown or Colonel Bland, to mention only a few of his sources, he observes:

May   14. Cherries ripe.
       16. First dish of peas from earliest patch.
       26. A second patch of peas come to table.
June   4. Windsor beans come to table.
        5. A third and fourth patch of peas come to table.
       13. A fifth patch of peas come in.
July   13. Last dish of peas.
       18. Last lettuce from Gehee's.
       23. Cucumbers from our garden.

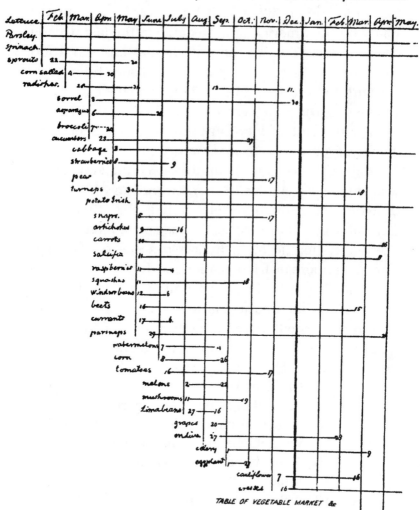

TABLE OF VEGETABLE MARKET &c

Aug.
    31. Watermelons from our patch.
     3. Indian corn comes to table.
       Black-eyed peas come to table.

Nov.
    16. The first frost sufficient to kill anything.

To a practical knowledge of the art of cookery Jefferson added a theoretical one. In his library, catalogued under the "Technical Arts" we find this imposing list of "cook books:"

The London Country Brewer, 8vo; Cimbrini's Theory and Practice of Brewing, 8vo; Knight on the Apple and Pear, Cider and Perry, 12mo; Apicii Coelius de opsoniis et Condimentis, sive Arte Coquinaria, 12mo. apud Waistburgios, Amerdam MDCCIX; Avis au peuple sur leur premier besoin (le pain) par l'Abbé Baudan, 12mo. Amsterdam MDCCLXXIV; Avis sur la manière de faire le pain, par Parmentier, 12mo; Le Parfait Boulanger, par Parmentier, Paris MDCCLXXVIII, 8vo; Parmentier sur les Pommes de Terre (learned treatise) Paris, MDCCLXXXI, 12mo; Eale's cookery, 12mo; Dictionaire Domestique, 30 12mo. Paris MDCCLXIV; Kraft's American Distiller, 8vo; Tracts on Potash & Maple Sugar, Williamos, Hopkins remarks on Maple Sugar, 8vo; Resultats de la Fabrication des Sirops et des Conserves de Raisins, par Parmentier, 8vo. Paris 1812.

During his travels in Europe Jefferson made a point of sampling the foods and fruits of the locality through which he was passing. Thus in Holland he first tasted waffles and promptly bought a waffle iron for 1.3 florins. In Amsterdam it was Hyson's tea that pleased him and he carried along half a pound for 2

florins 13. At Nancy he notes paying "1 franc 4 for
chocolate," and in his tour of southern France he
made a comparative gustatory study of oranges in the
various towns he visited. Ortolans, also came under
his notice; he paid 6 francs for a dozen of them at
Nice. At Rozzano he took elaborate notes on the
making of butter and Parmesan cheese and observed,
on sampling a frozen delicacy, that "snow gives the
most delicate flavor to creams, but ice is the most
powerful congealer and lasts longer." On his return to
the United States he found the luxuries to which he
had become accustomed sadly wanting, and Petit,
who followed him, was instructed to "bring a stock of
macaroni, Parmesan cheese, figs of Marseilles,
Brugnoles, raisins, almonds, mustard, vinaigre
d'Estragon, other good vinegar, oil and anchovies."

Jefferson was the first to introduce vanilla to this
country as well as macaroni. In 1791, when Secretary
of State, he wrote from Philadelphia to William Short,
the American chargé at Paris:

Petit informs me that he has been all over the town
in quest of vanilla, & it is unknown here. I must pray
you to send me a packet of 50 pods (batons) which
may come very well in the middle of a packet of
newspapers. It costs about 24 s a baton when sold
by the single baton. Petit says there is a great impo-
sition in selling those which are bad; that Piebot
generally sells good, but that still it will be safe to
have them bought by some one used to them.

It was a connoisseur of wines, however, that
Jefferson outshone all his contemporaries. He
regarded wine, to use his own words, "as a necessity

of life." "I rejoice as a moralist, he wrote toward the end of his life, "at the prospect of a reduction of the duties on wine, by our national legislature. It is an error to view a tax on that liquor as merely a tax on the rich. It is a prohibition of its use to the middling class of our citizens, and a condemnation of them to the poison of whiskey, which is desolating their houses. No nation is drunken where wine is cheap; and none sober, where the dearness of wine substitutes ardent spirits as the common beverage. It is, in truth, the only antidote to the bane of whiskey. Fix but the duty at the rate of other merchandise, and we can drink wine here as cheap as we do grog; and who will not prefer it? Its extended use will carry health and comfort to a much enlarged circle. Every one in easy circumstances (as the bulk of our citizens are) will prefer it to the poison to which they are now driven by their government. And the treasury itself will find that a penny apiece from a dozen, is more than a groat from a single one. This reformation, however, will require time."

During his travels through France and Germany in 1788, Jefferson made an extensive study of the vintages and the cultivation of grapes, not only for the sake of importing the wines, but also to introduce the culture to Virginia, something he had attempted even before the Revolution. From his faithful account book we observe that this was always in his thoughts. Thus he mentions, on April 10, 1788, at Hocheim, buying one hundred vines for 2f.15, and the same day, at Rudesheim, fifty vines for the same price. These were destined, of course, for America. The travel notes he

made at this time are a learned treatise on vinicul-
ture. Nothing is omitted, from the imposing list
beginning with Le Comte de Sichen, Le Comte
d'Oschenstein, L'Electeur de Mayence, Le Comte de
Meternisch, whose estates were said to yield the best
crops and which produced the famous Schloss
Johannisberger, to the important information that
"the vignerons of Rudesheim dung their vines about
once in five years, putting a one-horse tumbrel load of
dung on every twelve feet square."

It was thus no accident that Jefferson's friends
should come to rely upon his taste and knowledge. In
1790 we find him ordering sixty-five dozen bottles of
wine for the President, George Washington, and as
late as 1818 all but half a dozen lines of the letter of
congratulation he wrote the new President, James
Monroe, were devoted to a disquisition on the best
wines of the time for official entertaining.

During his own administration the President's
house was famous alike for its cuisine and its cellar.
The amount consumed was appalling, according to
our present standards. As usual Jefferson kept
careful account and made most detailed estimates.
He noted, on March 20, 1804, "there remain on hand
40 bottles of the 247 of champagne received from
Fulwer Skipwith December 1. The consumption, then
has been 207 bottles, which on 651 persons dined is
a bottle to 3 1/7 persons. Hence the annual stock
necessary may be calculated at 415 bottles a year, or
say 500."

The five hundred bottles of champagne were a mere
beginning. From a list of "wine provided at
Washington," preserved among the Jefferson papers,

we learn that in 1801 the President bought "five pipes of Brazil Madeira, a pipe of Pedo Ximenes Mountain (1269 gallons, 424 bottles of it sent to Monticello); a quarter cask of Tent; a keg of Pacharetté doux; 400 bottles of claret; 540 bottles of Sauterne." The record for the following years is no less magnificent.

Hospitality at the President's house during Jefferson's administration took on something of the free and easy character of a bachelor's establishment, and it was always on a lavish scale. While in France Jefferson had formed "the habit of mitigating business with dinner," to which he always afterwards adhered. He entertained informally at dinner every day at four o'clock. The company usually numbered fourteen and was, as a contemporary remarked, "selected in reference to their tastes, habits and suitability in all respects, which attempt had a wonderful effect in making his parties more agreeable than dinner parties usually are." A French cook reproduced many of the delicacies Jefferson had teamed in France, and added a number of his own. "Never before," one of his guests remarked, "had such dinners been given in the President's house, nor such a variety of the finest and most costly wines. In his entertainments republican simplicity was united with epicurean delicacy; while the absence of splendor, ornament and profusion was more than compensated by the neatness, order, and elegant sufficiency that pervaded the whole establishment. . . . "

It was left to a New England clergyman to complain that fried eggs and fried beef were served at the same dinner with turkey, ducks, and rounds of beef, but he was consoled by tasting for the first time "the new foreign dish, macaroni," by sampling ices and "a new kind of pudding, very porous and light, inside white as milk, and covered with cream sauce." This may well have been the very "Blanc Manger" for which Jefferson acquired the following recipe in Paris:

4 oz sweet almonds, with 5 or 6 bitter almonds

pour boiling water on them to take off the skin

put them in a mortar and beat them with a little cream

take them out of the mortar and liquify (delayer) them with cream little by little (peu à peu) stirring them

4 oz of sugar to be put in

have ready some isinglass (colle de poisson) say 1 oz dissolved in boiling water and pour it into the preceding mixture, stirring them well together

Strain it thro' a napkin, put it into a mould, and it is done.

In Jefferson's day, as now, the executive mansion boasted of two dining rooms, a large one on the northwest corner and a smaller one on the south front. It was here that Jefferson gathered his friends about him. The room was elaborately furnished, as an inventory in Jefferson's own hand assures us. There was an "elegant side board with pedestals and urn knife cases, a large Mahogany Dining Table in six pieces, a Small dining Table in three parts, a large Mahogany Square Table, two Glass Cases to contain the Silver and plated ware, an Oval breakfast Table, and fifteen chairs, black and gold." Chintz curtains, then the height of fashion, hung at the windows, and the walls were decorated with "two elegant Girandoles and two looking Glasses." The floor was covered by a canvas cloth, painted green. In Jefferson's own words, this was "laid down on the floor of the dining room when the table is set and taken up when the table is removed, merely to secure a very handsome floor from grease and the scouring which that necessitates."

Jefferson had a particular aversion to the presence of servants while he was at table, "believing," as one writer says, "that much of the domestic and even public discord was produced by the mutilated and misconstructed repetition of free conversation at dinner tables, by these mute but not inattentive listeners." To avoid this he had brought back from France the idea of the "dumb waiter," a sort of stand with shelves, containing everything for the dinner from beginning to end. This was placed between the guests and enabled them to serve themselves. There were five of these in the private dining room of the executive mansion. Jefferson went even farther than this, as we learn from one of his guests. "There was in his dining room an invention for introducing and removing the dinner without the opening and shutting of doors. A set of circular shelves were so contrived in the wall, that on touching a spring they turned into the room loaded with the dishes placed on them by the servants without the wall, and by the same process the removed dishes were conveyed out of the room."

Despite his distinguished position Jefferson was beset with many of the vexations familiar to every householder. It was, apparently, no more simple a matter to obtain a good cook in his day than it is in ours. Among his papers is a curious document in Jefferson's own hand, executed in Philadelphia not long before he resigned as Secretary of State, in which he agrees to set free one James Hastings, negro, provided the latter will return with him to Monticello and properly train a new cook. The agreement reads:

Having been at great expence in having James Hastings taught the art of cookery, desiring to befriend him, and to require from him as little in return as possible, I do hereby promise & declare, that if the said James shall go with me to Monticello in the course of the ensuing winter, when I go to reside there myself, and shall there continue until he shall have taught such person as I shall place under him for that purpose to be a good cook, this previous condition being performed, he shall be thereupon made free, and I will thereupon execute all proper instruments to make him free. Given under my hand and seal in the county of Philadelphia and the state of Pennsylvania this 15th day of September one thousand seven hundred and ninety three

Witness

Adrien Petit   TH. JEFFERSON

With his election to the Presidency Jefferson's domestic troubles began in earnest. Not only was he confronted with an unfinished and half furnished executive mansion, which he immediately set about furnishing in the latest manner, but he was obliged to build up another household staff in addition to the one at Monticello. He did not adopt what might have been the easiest, certainly, the cheapest way, and bring some of his numerous slaves to the White

House, but employed free whites whom he paid from his salary. Shortly before his inauguration we find him writing "Citizen" La Tombe, one of his French correspondents in Philadelphia:

". . . I find great difficulty in composing my household. . . . You know the importance of a good maître d'hôtel in a large house and the impossibility of finding one among the natives of our country. I have imagined that such a person might be found, perhaps, among the French of Philadelphia, that no one would be more likely to know it than yourself, and that no one would be a better judge of his qualifications. Honesty and skill in making the dessert are indispensable qualifications, that he should be good humoured and of a steady, discreet disposition is also important. If there be such a one within the compass of your knowledge will you have the goodness to engage him to come to me immediately? . . . . I have a good cook, but it is *pour L'offce,* & to take charge of the family that I am distressed."

That Jefferson's difficulties were not at an end, and that the "good cook" apparently gave notice upon surveying the lack of facilities in the half-finished White House we may gather from the appeal made to the Chevalier d'Yrugo, the Spanish Minister to the United States: "I have understood that twenty dollars a month is what is given to the best French cook," Jefferson writes, "however, the Chevalier d'Yrugo, having been so kind as to undertake to get the one which he deemed the best in Philadelphia, I authorized him to go as high as twenty-eight dollars."

Thanks to the efforts of Citizen La Tombe and the Spanish Minister, a staff of eleven servants was presently organized, Joseph Rapin was engaged as maître d'hôtel, at $62.27 per month, although he was presently succeeded by Etienne Lemaire, who demanded only twenty dollars; one Julien became chef, at twenty-five dollars, and Noël, the garçon de cuisine, received eight. Edy and Fanny, two slaves from Monticello, were taken to the White House to learn French cooking, and when Jefferson finally retired to Monticello they became his cooks there. During his Washington days it was no uncommon sight early in the morning to see the President drive with his maitre d'hôtel to the market in Georgetown and take a hand in selecting the provisions for the day.

The cost of Jefferson's table was very great, even for that time, and in spite of his careful calculations. During the first year of his presidency, his income failed to meet the expenditures. In an analysis he made on March 4, 1802, we find that he had spent $4,504,84 for provisions, $2,003.71 for groceries, $2,797.28 for wines, to say nothing of $2,675.84 for his servants. Lemaire frequently spent fifty dollars upon a single day's marketing. In addition to the supplies purchased in Alexandria, Georgetown, and Richmond, things were constantly being sent from Monticello. Jefferson himself always ordered the provisions that were purchased on a large scale for the President's House, as well as for Monticello. Entertaining never ceased, even when he took his holiday. It is interesting to note what was required on the plantation for Jefferson's annual spring visit:

two pipes Marsalla; two casks Bucellas and Termo; five casks 50 doz. porter; 40 beef's tongues;

100 ham of Col. Mason; 4 kegs tomp and sounds, 40 lb. crackers; 5 bottles anchovies, 3 do pickles, 10 lb. almonds in a bag; 2 oz. cinnamon, 2 oz. nutmeg; 1 lb. allspice 1 lb. pepper; 6 bottles mustard; 6 lb. chocolate, 6 lb. sugar; 20 1/2 good cheese, 11 3/4 lb. ordinary; 40 lb. coffee; 10 lb. rice, 10 lb. pearl barley; 25 lb. raisins; 1 box sausages.

It is small wonder that such lavish entertaining should have made great inroads upon Jefferson's fortune. There were few men in America at the time who could have borne the burden, least of all a Virginia planter whose land was decreasing in value with every year. With his frugal New England outlook John Adams once remarked: "I dined a large company once or twice a week. Jefferson dined a dozen every day. I held levees once a week. Jefferson's whole eight years was a levee." John Adams had failed to understand the hospitality of the South, a hospitality by which Jefferson was quite literally eaten out of house and home.

When Jefferson ended his second term as President in 1808, and retired to Monticello, he was, for the first time since his earliest youth, able to lead the life he had always wished—that of a Virginia country gentleman. He was, to be sure, sixty-five years of age, but in his case it may very truly be said that he was sixty-five years young. He was to have eighteen years still before him, and he enjoyed them as he enjoyed perhaps, no other period of his life. His daughter, Martha Jefferson Randolph, presided over his household in the place of the wife he had lost so long ago, and his numerous grandchildren formed, in truth, a second family. He was as solicitous about their training and education as he had been about that of his own daughters. He had written to his own Polly, while Secretary of State, "I am much pleased with the account you give me of your occupations, and the making of the pudding is as good an article of them as any. When I come to Virginia I shall insist on eating a pudding of your own making, as well as on trying other specimens of your skill." He found time, as President, to send similar communications to each little granddaughter as she reached the age when the domestic virtues were to be cultivated. He suggested the books they read and the subjects they study; he was constantly sending them clippings of verse or other things of interest from the magazines and papers that passed through his hands, for them to paste in the scrapbooks he taught them to keep, and on resuming family life again at Monticello he talked with them about their books and the progress of their studies.

The Duke de la Rochefoucauld-Liancourt, whom Jefferson knew in France and who was a visitor at Monticello, has left an amiable picture of Jefferson as the master of Monticello: "In private life Mr. Jefferson displays a mild, easy, and obliging temper, though he is somewhat cold and reserved. His conversation is of the most agreeable kind, and he possesses a stock of information not inferior to that of any other man. In Europe he would hold a distinguished rank among men of letters, and as such he has already appeared there. At present he is employed with activity and perseverance in the management of his farms and buildings; and he orders, directs, and pursues in the minutest details every branch of business relative to them. I found him in the midst of the harvest, from which the scorching heat of the sun does not prevent his attendance. His negroes are nourished, clothed, and treated as well as white servants could be. As he can not expect any assistance from the two small neighboring towns, every article is made on his farm: his negroes are cabinet makers, carpenters, masons, bricklayers, smiths, etc. The children he employs in a nail factory, which yields already a considerable profit. The young and old negresses; spin for the clothing of the rest. He animates them by rewards and distinctions; in fine, his superior mind directs the management of his domestic concerns with the same abilities, activity, and regularity which he evinced in the conduct of public affairs, and which he is calculated to display in every situation of life."

The busy day at Monticello began with a nine o'clock breakfast at which all the family and guests assembled. Jefferson had been up since dawn, busy, with his correspondence. After breakfast, which was of the sturdy, Virginia variety—Daniel Webster mentions having hot breads and cold meats—with bacon and eggs and fried apples, and with the batter-cake express running at full speed between the kitchen and dining room, Jefferson visited his flower beds and garden, always in the company of several of his grandchildren. He then retired to his library, where he worked until one o'clock. At this hour his horse was brought and he rode about the plantation for an hour or two. Dinner was served at half-past three o'clock, "in half Virginian, half French style, in good taste and abundance," Webster remarks. At six o'clock coffee and tea were brought to the drawing room. "He sat some time at table," one of his granddaughters writes, "and after dinner returned for a while to his room, from which he emerged before sunset, to walk on the terrace or the lawn, to see his grandchildren run races, or to converse with his family and friends. The evenings, after candle-light, he passed with us, till about ten o'clock. He had his own chair and his own candle, a little apart from the rest, where he sat reading, if there were no guests to require his attention, but often laying his book on his little round table or his knee, while he talked with my mother." Jefferson's reading chair and table were by the fireplace in the dining room, where the family seems to have spent a good deal of time, especially in winter. The dining room, just to the right of the sunny drawing room, where the mornings were passed when guests were present, opens on to a semi-octagonal tea room, in which dinner was frequently served.

When Jefferson retired to Monticello his daughter is said to have asked him on what scale he wished to live, and he is supposed to have answered: "I will live like a plain country gentleman." It did not take him long to discover that this was to be impossible. The American public of the early nineteenth century took quite as much interest in its ex-presidents as the public of today, even more so in the case of the distinguished author of the Declaration of Independence. The visitors to Monticello were legion; they assumed something of the proportions of a bonus army. As one of Jefferson's granddaughters said of them: "They came of all nations, at all times, and paid longer or shorter visits. I have known a New England judge to bring a letter of introduction to my grandfather, and stay three weeks. The learned Abbé Correa, always a welcome guest, passed some weeks of each year with us during the whole time of his stay in the country. We had persons from abroad, from all the States of the Union, from every part of the State—men, women, and children. In short, almost every day, for at least eight months of the year, brought its contingent of guests. People of wealth, fashion, men in office, professional men, military and civil, lawyers, doctors, Protestant clergymen, Catholic priests, members of Congress, foreign ministers, missionaries, Indian agents, tourists, travellers, artists, strangers, friends. Some came from affection and respect, some from curiosity, some to give or receive advice or instruction, some from idleness, some because others set the example, and very varied, amusing, and agreeable was the society afforded by this influx of guests. I have listened to very remarkable conversations carried on round the table, the fireside, or in the summer drawing-room. . . .

"There were few eminent men of our country, except perhaps, some political adversaries, who did not visit him in his retirement, to say nothing of distinguished foreigners. Life at Monticello was on an easy and informal footing. Mr. Jefferson always made his appearance at an early breakfast, but his mornings were most commonly devoted to his own occupations, and it was at dinner, after dinner, and in the evening, that he gave himself up to the society of his family and his guests. Visitors were left free to employ themselves as they liked during the morning hours—to walk, read, or seek companionship with the ladies of

the family and each other. M. Correa passed his time
in the fields and the woods; some gentlemen preferred
the library; others the drawing-room; others the quiet
of their own chambers; or they strolled down the
mountain side and under the shade of the trees. The
ladies in like manner consulted their ease and inclinations, and whiled away the time as best they
might."

As there were no near-by taverns, and furthermore,
as it was the custom of the country to ask a visitor to
have a meal, if not to spend the night, Jefferson was
soon in a position to feel about Monticello much as
Washington once expressed himself about Mount
Vernon—that his home was a well-resorted inn.
Within two years of Jefferson's retirement it was found
necessary to employ thirtyseven house servants at
Monticello, and the whole estate was unable to
furnish enough food for the guests, their servants and
horses. It is said that Mrs. Randolph, upon whose
capable shoulders the burden of this vast amount of
entertaining rested, once observed that fifty unex-
pected guests was the largest number she had ever
been called upon to house overnight. "I have never
seen her at all disturbed by any amount of care or
trouble," the overseer of Monticello was able to
remark after knowing her and serving her for more
than twenty years.

The tradition of fine cooking was carried on at
Monticello, as it had been at the White House, and
inherited by Jefferson's grandchildren. Each of the six
granddaughters, as thoroughly schooled in the
domestic arts as in French, Latin, or music, carefully

copied, in the delicate hand writing they had learned from their mother, the favorite "rules" and "receipts" of the household, whether from Lemaire, the President's steward, from Julien, the chef, Petit, the old stand-by, Annette, or some friend. Sometimes they were taken from a receipt book much used in the family. The pages of these hand-written cook books are neatly bound together in little volumes, if they may so be called, with a bit of slender but carefully tied cord. There is a "volume" on soups, one on "Made Dishes," a third on "Creams etc." and a fourth on puddings. Greatly prized, these Monticello cook books were carried by the brides of the family to their new homes, as one of their greatest treasures.

To the present-day cook some of the receipts may seem incredibly archaic and amusing, as, for example, the one for chocolate or coffee cream. This was nothing more than elaborate junket, but instead of reaching casually for a junket tablet and preparing the dessert in less than five minutes, the skill of two persons was involved and much preparation in advance. The directions read:

Put on your milk, 1 quart to 2 squares of chocolate; boil it away one quarter. Take it off, let it cool and sweeten it. Lay a napkin in a bowl, put three gizzards in the napkin and pass the cream through it four times, as quick as possible, one person rubbing the gizzards with a spoon while another pours. Put it in cups and set the cups in cold water half way up their sides. Set the water on the fire, cover it, and put fire on the top. As soon as the water boils, take the cups out and set them to cool.

The gizzards used for this purpose are only the inside skins, taken off as soon as the chicken is killed, washed, dried, and kept in paper bags in a dry place. The effect is the same with rennet.

The book of Monticello recipes here reproduced is the one made by Virginia Randolph, Martha Jefferson Randolph's fifth daughter, who was born in 1801 and who, in 1821 , married Nicholas P. Trist, later our envoy to Mexico. On her death it passed to her only daughter, Martha Jefferson Trist, and subsequently to the latter's daughter, Fanny M. Burke of Alexandria. Miss Burke presented the book to the Thomas Jefferson Memorial Foundation, shortly before her death, and joined with the Foundation in giving the editor permission to prepare it for publication. As here given the recipes are adapted for modem use—the dozen eggs and pound of butter common to an earlier era being not only appalling in quantity, but terrifying in price to the householder of the present day. They have been proportioned to our current practice of a formula for serving six persons, and the directions for cooking, or baking, or boiling, as the case may be, have been adapted and tested to suit an electric or gas stove, rather than meet exigencies of cooking over a crane or submitting one's chef d'oeuvre to the questionable mercies of a hot shovel or poker. Gelatine has been substituted for calves' hoofs, junket for chicken gizzard, and our useful American food chopper for mortar and pestle.

THOMAS JEFFERSON'S PARIS RECIPES

ICE CREAM

Beat the yolks of 6 eggs until thick and lemon colored. Add, gradually, 1 cup of sugar and a pinch of salt. Bring to a boil 1 quart of cream and pour slowly on the egg mixture. Put in top of double boiler and when it thickens, remove and strain through a fine sieve into a bowl. When cool add 2 teaspoonfuls of vanilla. Freeze, as usual, with one part of salt to three parts of ice. Place in a mould, pack in ice and salt for several hours. For electric refrigerators, follow usual direction, but stir frequently.

BLANC MANGE

Blanch and remove skins from 1/4 pound almonds, along with 5 or 6 bitter almonds. Put through food chopper, using finest grinder. Add gradually, stirring constantly, 2 cups thin cream. Stir in 3 tablespoonfuls of sugar, and a few grains of salt. Soak 1 scant tablespoonful of gelatine in 2 table-spoonfuls cold water for five minutes. Dissolve in 1/4 cup of boiling water. Add to almond mixture, stirring well together. Strain through a fine sieve, pour into moulds, "and it is done."

WINE JELLY

Soak 2 tablespoonfuls of gelatine in 1/2 cup water for five minutes. Dissolve in 1 pint of milk that has been brought to a boil. Add 3/4 cup of sugar and pinch of salt, let cool. Add 1 pint of Madeira wine and the juice of 3 lemons. Add more sugar if not sufficiently sweet. Strain through a double cheesecloth and pour into moulds.

BISCUIT DE SAVOYE

Separate 6 eggs. Beat the yolks until lemon colored and light. Add 6 tablespoonfuls of sugar and the grated rind of one orange. Beat well; add 6 tablespoonfuls of sifted flour mixed with 1/8 teaspoonful of salt. Beat the egg whites until stiff and dry. Fold into the first mixture. Butter a cake mould and dust with sugar. Turn the mixture into this and set in a slow oven. Bake from thirty to forty minutes, or until cake shrinks from edge of pan.

MACAROONS

Pour boiling water on 1 pound of almonds and remove the skin. Wash them in cold water. Wipe them well with a towel. Put them through a food chopper, using finest grinder. Turn into a wooden bowl and add gradually 3/4 of a pound of powdered sugar, beating thoroughly all the while with a wooden spoon. Add, one by one, the whites of 3 eggs, beating constantly to a smooth paste. Drop from the tip of a spoon on white paper, in small balls about the size of a nut. Bake fifteen to twenty minutes in a slow oven.

MERINGUES

Beat the whites of 6 eggs to a stiff froth. Add, very gradually, 6 tablespoonfuls of sugar. With a tablespoon form them into rounds of desired size, on a piece of white paper. Put in a very slow oven. You may leave them there as long as you wish.

NOODLES À LA MACARONI

Beat 6 eggs until light, add 1 cup milk and 1/2 teaspoon salt. Add enough flour, about 4 cups, to make a thick dough. Roll, with a rolling pin, to 1/8-inch thickness. Cut into small pieces and roll these between the hands into long strips resembling macaroni. Cut them to a proper length. Drop into boiling, salted water and cook for fifteen minutes. Dress them as you would macaroni. They may also be served boiled in soup.

BRANDIED PEACHES

Wipe off the peaches to remove the down. Prick them in four or five places with a fork. Drop them into boiling water for a moment, remove, and place immediately in cold water. Remove and let them drain. Make a syrup of sugar and a little water, using one pound of sugar to four pounds of peaches. Boil until, when you dip two fingers into it, they will stick together. Let cool. Add the peaches and let stand for twenty-four hours. Bring the syrup to a boil again and add 1 pint of brandy. Do not leave the syrup on the fire while you are doing this. You will bum your face if you do not take this precaution. Let the syrup cool again and add the peaches. The following day remove the peaches again, bring syrup to a boil and add as much brandy as you wish. Put in the peaches and let simmer until tender. Let them cool, then remove gently and put in jars. Strain the syrup over them through a cheesecloth.

THE MONTICELLO RECIPES

SOUPS

OBSERVATIONS ON SOUPS

Always observe to lay your meat in the bottom of the pan with a lump of butter. Cut the herbs and vegetables very fine and lay over the meat. Cover it close and set over a slow fire. This will draw the virtue out of the herbs and roots and give the soup a different flavour from what it would have from putting the water in at first. When the gravy produced from the meat is almost dried up, fill your pan up with water. When your soup is done, take it up and when cool enough, skim off the grease quite clean. Put it on again to heat and then dish it up. When you make white soups, never put in the cream until you take it off the fire. Soup is better the second day in cool weather.

Monticello.

BEEF SOUP

Take a shin of beef, or any offal piece, cut it up and fry it a light brown in 2 tablespoonfuls of butter, stirring it frequently to prevent its burning. Cover it entirely with water and let it come to a boil. Skim the foam that rises and boil slowly until the meat is tender and falls apart, adding more water, should it boil away too much. Take 3 onions, a small cabbage, 2 turnips, 2 parsnips, a stalk of celery and cut them in small, even pieces. Melt 3 tablespoonfuls of butter in a pan, add the vegetables and turn them over and over in the butter until well coated. Cover with some of the broth from the soup and cook slowly until thoroughly done. Season with salt and a very little pepper. Mix the whole together and serve.

The cabbage should not be put in until after the other vegetables are almost done, as it takes a shorter time to fry.

Monticello.

NOODLES TO THICKEN THE SOUP

Beat 3 eggs slightly, add 1/2 cup milk, 2 cups flour, 1/2 teaspoonful of salt. Mix together well. It should form a stiff dough. If necessary, add more flour. Roll out very thin, cut in small pieces, which roll again in long strips. They should be very thin. Then cut them again in strips about 2 inches long and 1/4 of an inch wide and put them in the soup. If you mean to dress them as macaroni, drop them in boiling water, cover fifteen minutes and drain.

SOUP À LA JULIENNE

Take carrots, turnips and potatoes and cut them in strips about 3/4 of an inch long and 1/12 of an inch wide. There should be 3/4 cupful of each. Melt 2 tablespoonfuls of butter, add the vegetables and fry gently, stirring carefully, until they begin to shrivel. Then put them in the soup. When it boils, add 1/4 cup of sorrel, and 1/2 cup of spinach, which should first have been scalded with boiling water to take the sharpness out, then drain and chop fine. Add to your julienne also 3 stalks of celery and 2 beets cut up like turnips and carrots. Also 1/2 cup of green peas, when they are in season.

This soup should be made with beef broth, about

21/2 quarts, or if water is used 3 spoonfuls of dried beans that have been soaked should be put in.

It should cook for two hours. Before serving cut 3 slices of bread in small cubes and brown in butter. Add to soup.

Annette.

MEXICAN BEAN SOUP

To 3 quarts of water add 1 pint of black Mexican beans that have been thoroughly washed, and 2 pounds of shortribs of beef or a veal knuckle. Boil slowly for three to four hours, until the beans are soft. Pour through a colander and press the beans through. Simmer again for fifteen minutes, add salt and pepper to taste. Serve with small squares of bread that have been toasted and browned in butter. If intended for mock turtle soup, add a small glass of wine.

Receipt furnished by the grocer who sold the beans.

PUMPKIN SOUP

Take half a small pumpkin, peel, cut in small pieces and put on the stove with half a glass of water. When the pumpkin is tender, drain, and pass through a colander. Add 3 tablespoonfuls of butter; sugar, salt, and pepper to taste. Let it simmer for fifteen minutes. Add 4 cups boiling milk, stirring well while pouring it in. When well mixed, pour over croutons, made by cutting three slices of bread in small cubes and browning well in butter.

Annette.

POTATO SOUP

Peal and cut 3 large potatoes in pieces. Cover with water and boil until tender. Put through a colander and add 3 cups of water. Bring to a boil, add salt to taste, 2 tablespoonfuls of butter, 1/4 cup rice or a tablespoonful of tapioca. Cook for twenty-five minutes. Add 1 tablespoonful of sorrel, chopped fine. Beat the yolks of 3 eggs until light, add to the soup and serve.

Annette.

Where eggs are put into soup they should not be put into the pot on the fire, but after it has been removed. Tomatoes are a very good substitute for sorrel.

PEA SOUP

Take 1 cup of green peas, drop into 2 1/2 cups of boiling, salted water. Cook until tender. Drain, but keep the water for the soup. Pass peas through colander, add to water with 1/2 teaspoonful of sugar, 1/2 tablespoonful of chopped sorrel or parsley, or any other green vegetable, and thicken with 1 tablespoonful of flour mixed to a paste with 1 tablespoonful of butter. Add well beaten yolks of 2 eggs.

All other kinds of soup 'a la puree are made in the same manner, but if made of dry vegetables they should be put in cold water.

Annette.

GUMBO

One quart of okra, 1 quart of tomatoes, 1 pound of any kind of meat, but veal or chicken is best. Cut up the meat in small pieces and roll in flour. Put a large tablespoonful of butter into the soup pot and fry the meat until brown. Cut up 1 large onion and fry brown. Then add the okra that has been cut up, also the tomatoes peeled and cut in small pieces and fry brown. Let all cook together for fifteen minutes. Add 2 quarts of water; salt, pepper and herbs to taste. Cook four or five hours, stirring frequently. A pod of green pepper, cut up and added is a great improvement.

Mrs. G. W. Randolph.

Gumbo may be made with sassafras leaves dried and powdered, instead of okra, but the sassafras leaves must not be put in until the soup is done. Then add 2 tablespoonfuls of sassafras.

OKRA SOUP

Cut up 1 quart of okra, add 2 cups of water and bring to a boil. Half an hour later add 1 cup of lima beans, a pound of fresh meat cut up, or a fowl. An hour before serving add 5 tomatoes cut in pieces. When almost done put in a lump of butter as big as an egg, rolled in flour. Do not make it too thick. Put it on early and only let it simmer.

Mrs. Martha Randolph, Monticello.

OKRA SOUP

Take the okra so young as to be crisp, about two or three inches long. They may be used as long as they are tender, which may be judged by their brittleness. If good, they snap; if they bend, they are too old. Slice

1 quart like cucumbers for eating, 1/2 inch thick. Add 1/3 the amount of tomatoes, more or less according to taste, a shin of beef, and 3 quarts of water. You may add 3 ears of young corn cut from the cob, and 2 cups of lima beans. The soup should boil for five hours. It will be reduced to one-half. When done, the meat will be boiled to rags and quit the bone. The whole should be one homogeneous mass, in which none of the ingredients should be distinct. Its consistency should be just as thick as porridge; the color green, mixed with yellow or red from the tomatoes.

University of Virginia.

CATFISH SOUP

To 2 quarts of water, add 4 or 5 catfish, according to size, a slice of lean ham, 2 onions chopped fine, 3 sprigs of parsley, a bunch of sweet herbs, half a dozen peppercorns, and a teaspoonful of salt. Boil until the fish go to pieces, strain, put on fire again with another fish that has been skinned and cut in pieces. Boil until fish is tender. Add 1/2 pint cream, 1 tablespoonful of flour, mixed to a paste with 2 tablespoonfuls of butter, and the yolks of 4 eggs. Serve with chopped parsley.

OYSTER SOUP

Stew 3 slices of bacon and 3 sprigs of parsley with a pint of water, and 1 quart of oysters which have been washed and drained. Stew for half an hour. Add

1 pint of cream, 3 tablespoonfuls of butter rolled in flour, and the yolks of 2 eggs.

Mrs. Martha Randolph.

MUTTON BROTH

Takes 2 pounds of neck of mutton, wash it very well, let it soak in cold water one hour. Put it in a soup pot with 3 quarts of water and bring to a boil. Skim as often as the foam rises. Add 1/2 pint of barley. Let simmer for four hours, Two hours before serving add the vegetables, 6 carrots, 3 stalks celery, 2 turnips, 1 onion, cut in fine pieces. Should the water boil away too much, add more, according to your own judgment. The salt and pepper you put in must be after your own taste.

When done, take out all the bones of the mutton, and the meat, which will, by this time, be done to rags.

Ellen Wayles Randolph Coolidge.

BEAN SOUP

Put 2 cups of beans to soak in water to cover at night. The next morning put them into a pot with 1 teaspoonful of salt and 2 quarts of water. Bring to a boil and simmer slowly for an hour. Then add 6 carrots, 2 turnips, and 1 parsnip, scraped and cut into small, even pieces. Let the soup simmer for three or four hours, skimming when necessary. When the vegetables are soft press the whole through a colander and return to the pot. Scrape and cut 4 stalks of celery into small pieces and add to the soup. Let simmer until tender. If the soup gets too thick add enough boiling water to make of proper consistency. Cut 4 slices of bread into small pieces, toast, and turn over and over in butter. Pour the soup over this and serve.

Gouverneur Morris the Elder.

PIGEON SOUP

Cut up 2 pigeons and put into 2 quarts of water, let simmer three hours. Strain, and put juice back into soup kettle with 4 sprigs of parsley and 1/2 cupful of spinach, finely chopped. Add 1 pint of cream in which 1/2 cupful of bread crumbs have been mixed. Cut up the pigeon meat in small pieces, season with salt and a little mace, and simmer in the soup for fifteen minutes.

Mrs. Horace Mann.

STOCK FOR CLEAR SOUP

Cut up a knuckle of veal into small pieces. Place into a soup pot with 4 tablespoonfuls of butter and 3 teaspoonfuls of salt, 1/2 dozen peppercorns, 3 small onions sliced, 2 cloves, 6 carrots, 2 leeks, 1 turnip, 4 stalks of celery. To add more zest to the flavor add the smallest quantity of thyme, 1 1/4 teaspoonfuls winter savory in the same amount, and a bay leaf. Add 1 cup of water, set on stove and bring to a boil. When boiling stir for ten minutes, or until it forms a whitish, thick gravy at the bottom, or gets rather dry. Then add 5 pints of water. When it comes to a boil, let it simmer for 3/4 of an hour. Stir it well, strain it through a cheesecloth and it will be found clear and ready for use. Take the fat off.

Soyer.

WHITE SOUP

Put into a bowl 1/2 cup of flour, stir in slowly 1 cup of milk, 1/2 teaspoonful salt, 1/4 teaspoonful pepper. Add gradually to the broth (in the quantity of the preceding recipe for stock). Boil gently for ten minutes, stirring constantly. Skim it. It may be poured over the veal, or have some more of the vegetables that were used in the stock, added. They should be cut small, fried, and simmered in the soup. Remove any fat. You may add a cup of rice, or macaroni, or vermicelli, previously boiled until tender. Fried or toasted bread, cut in dice, may be added.

Soyer.

A FRENCH SOUP MAIGRE

Take a large lump of butter and a tablespoonful of flour. Brown them in the saucepan in which the soup is to be made. Chop until fine 6 carrots, 2 onions, 4 stalks of celery, 2 potatoes, and some sorrel. Mix them together, put them into the saucepan, add pepper and salt to taste, and pour on boiling water until generously covered. Let them stew for three or four hours. They can hardly simmer too long. A little thyme, parsley, cress and mint are a great improvement, added to the above ingredients.

VEGETABLE PORRIDGE

Scrape and peel the following vegetables: 6 carrots, 6 turnips, 6 onions, 3 heads of celery, and 3 parsnips. Slice very thinly and put into a soup pot with 6 tablespoonfuls of butter. Add a bunch of parsley, a large sprig of thyme and fill the pot with water, about 4 quarts. Set on stove. Season to taste with salt and pepper. Boil very slowly for two hours. At the end of this time the vegetables will be cooked to a pulp. Press all through a colander with a wooden spoon. Return to pot and bring to a boil. Serve.

POT AU FEU

Take 3 pounds of beef, the short ribs are best, put in a soup kettle and cover well with cold water, about 3 quarts, and bring to a boil. Skim well. Add 1 table-spoonful of salt, 2 large carrots, 2 turnips, 1 parsnip, 3 large onions, each one with a clove stuck in it, a small piece of garlic, a bunch of leeks, and a small stalk of celery. Let it boil very slowly for five or six hours.

Annette.

GUMBO

Put 2 tablespoonfuls of fat in a skillet and stir in gradually 1 tablespoonful of flour, 1 teaspoonful of chopped parsley and 1/2 an onion minced fine. When the flour is brown, add 1 fowl which has been disjointed, and let it brown. Add 4 pints of water and season with salt, black and red pepper. Let it boil gently for an hour and a half. Just before serving stir in, while stirring constantly, 2 or 3 tablespoonfuls of gumbo (sassafras leaves, dried and pounded) according to the amount of liquid in the pot. Do not let boil after the gumbo is put in. Turn into soup tureen and serve.

Mrs. Rosella Trist.

MEATS AND FOWL

IMPORTANT OBSERVATIONS ON ROASTING, BOILING, AND FRYING

In roasting, the meat should be washed and wiped dry, sprinkled with salt and a little pepper, dredged with flour and put in a very hot oven. When the flour in the pan begins to brown, add a tablespoonful of shortening and baste the meat every ten minutes. Reduce the heat. Put 1/2 cup of water in pan and continue basting until meat is done and a nice, brown crust formed.

Beef and mutton must not be roasted as much as veal) lamb or pork. Veal may be served with a little melted butter on the platter, but all the others must be served without sauce. For those who must have gravy with these meats, let it be made in any way they like and served in a boat. A loin of lamb or a hindquarter of lamb should be served with the kidneys about the platter.

Whatever is to be boiled must be put in cold water with a little salt. When they are put in boiling water the outside is done too much before the inside is heated.

In choosing meat you must see that the fat is not yellow and that the lean parts are of a fine, close grain, a lively color, and will feel tender when pinched. Poultry should be well covered with white fat. If the bottom of the breastbone be gristly, it is young; but if a hard bone, it is an old one.

For broiling, sprinkle with a little salt and pepper and put broiler under a hot flame. When done, put on platter, pour over some melted butter and chopped parsley. This is for broiled veal, wild fowl, birds or poultry. Beefsteak and mutton chops require only a tablespoonful of hot water poured over.

To have viands served in perfection, the dishes should be made hot, either by setting them over hot water, or by putting some in them.

RULES TO BE OBSERVED IN MADE DISHES

If cream is to be used in them it must never be suffered to boil after it is put in, for fear of its turning.

Lemon juice or mushroom pickle should be put in just as you are about to serve them, otherwise they will curdle. The sauce should be smooth and of the thickness of cream.

Made dishes with a brown sauce should be a good thickness.

Care must be taken in seasoning that no one article should predominate and that your dish should be free from scum and fat.

Martha Jefferson Randolph.

A WHITE FRICASSEE

Take 2 chickens, skin them, cut the joints asunder and lay them in warm water for fifteen minutes. Dry them and stew them slowly in half milk, half water, until tender. To 1 cup of milk and 1 cup of cream add 4 tablespoonfuls of butter. Simmer until thick. Cool, add a dash of mace, 1/2 nutmeg grated, 1/2 teaspoonful of salt, 1/2 cup of white wine and 1 cup of mushrooms. Stir well. Remove chickens from the liquor in which they were cooked, discard that, put chickens in the gravy and heat thoroughly. Serve.

Lamb, tripe and rabbits may be dressed the same way.

Mrs. Martha Randolph.

TO STEW RABBITS, CHICKENS OR DUCKS

Take a rabbit. Put a bunch of parsley and an onion in its belly. Parboil. Cut into pieces. Take the onion, parsley and liver and shred fine. Mix 3 tablespoonfuls of claret or Madeira with 1/2 of vinegar, and dissolve 2 anchovies in it. Put into the stewpan with a little of the liquor in which they were boiled. When tender thicken with 1 tablespoonful of butter rolled in flour.

Martha Jefferson Randolph.

FRICASSEE OF CHICKEN

Cut 2 young chickens in pieces and put them in hot water. Let stand ten minutes. Remove the chickens, dry carefully and strain the water. Put 3 good tablespoonfuls of water in a saucepan and turn the chickens well in it. Add a tablespoonful of flour, stir well, and add the water in which the chickens were scalded. Simmer one-half hour. Add 6 small onions, a dozen mushrooms and a bunch of herbs. When the onions and mushrooms are done, the chickens ought to be done, also. Remove the chickens to a platter, add the yolks of 2 eggs to the gravy stirring vigorously. Pour over the chicken and serve. You can, if you like, beat in the juice of a lemon with the egg.

Annette.

CHICKEN WITH RICE

Put your chicken into a casserole with 2 small onions which have doves stuck into them, 3 carrots cut in fine slices, a bunch of parsley and some bits of veal, if you have any. Pour some stock on the chicken and vegetables until nearly covered. Cook gently for 2 hours. When the fowl is done pour the broth through a sieve and boil 6 tablespoonfuls of rice in it until tender. Put the chicken in the middle of a platter and surround with rice.

Annette.

CHICKEN À LA MERENGO

Cut up a fowl and brown in oil. Add 1 cupful of button mushrooms; salt, and pepper to taste, a very small piece of garlic, 1 teaspoonful of chopped parsley, a tablespoonful of chopped tomatoes or tomato sauce, a tablespoonful of meat jelly, and the juice of 1 lemon. Let simmer until the fowl is tender. If the sauce gets too dry, add a little water as it cooks.

*CAPITOLADE OF THE REMAINS OF ROAST FOWL

Cut leftover pieces of fowl in small, even pieces. Put 2 tablespoonfuls of butter in a frying pan, add the fowl and stir well. Fry it with some chopped herbs and add 1 tablespoonful of flour, 1 cup of chicken gravy, and 1 wineglassful of white wine. Add salt to taste. Simmer for ten minutes. This dish is for breakfast.

Annette.

*A ragout of cold meat.

PIGEONS IN COMPOTE

Take 4 good pigeons, draw them, wash well, dry and dust with salt and pepper. Make a brown gravy with stock and put your pigeons to cook in it for one and a half hours over a low fire. At the end of the first half-hour, add 2 sprigs of parsley, 1 cup of mushrooms, sliced, and 4 or 5 very small onions. The sauce should be thick.

Annette.

PIGEONS À LA COMPOTE

Split two pigeons through the stomach and flatten the backs with a bread knife. Broil for twenty-five minutes, taking care that they are evenly browned. Serve with tartar sauce. This dish is generally used for breakfast.

Annette.

CIVET OF HARE

Melt 3 tablespoonfuls of butter and fry in it 12 small onions that have been carefully peeled. When a delicate brown, remove from the butter and add 1 1/2 tablespoonfuls of flour. Stir well together. Add 1 hare which has been disjointed and stir in the butter mixture for five minutes. Add 1 1/2 cups of white wine and 1 1/2 cups of stock, salt and pepper to taste, and 3 sprigs of parsley. When the hare is nearly done, put back the onions and add 1 cup of button mushrooms.

Annette.

CROQUETTES OF ROASTED VEAL

Put some roasted veal through a food chopper. There should be 2 cupfuls. Put 3 tablespoonfuls of butter in a saucepan with chopped herbs to taste, and simmer a few minutes. Add 1/3 cup of flour, stir well; add 1 cup of stock. Season to taste with salt and pepper. Add the chopped veal. Remove from fire and shape into balls. Let stand until cold. Dip into melted butter, then into crumbs, then into egg, again in crumbs. Then fry them.

Annette.

BRAISED LEG OF MUTTON

Bone a leg of mutton and lard it with fine strips of bacon. Rub with salt, pepper and any desired herbs, such as thyme. Put together with skewers so as to make it appear it is not boned. Put 3 tablespoonfuls of butter in a saucepan and brown the meat in this. When a good color, add 3 cups of stock, 3 carrots cut lengthwise in strips, 3 onions, each with a clove stuck in it, 3 sprigs of parsley and the bones of your leg of mutton. Cover and let simmer four hours. If the sauce is too thin when you go to serve it, thicken with a little flour.

Annette.

HASH OF BRAISED OR ROASTED LEG OF MUTTON

Melt 3 tablespoonfuls of butter in a saucepan and 1 teaspoonful of shallot chopped fine and fry for five minutes over a low flame. Add 1 tablespoonful of flour, 1 cup of stock, 1/2 teaspoonful of salt and 1 teaspoonful of vinegar. Let it simmer for twenty minutes.

Have 2 cups of mutton cut up in small pieces, very neat, and let them heat in your sauce without boiling.

Annette.

BRAISED MUTTON CHOPS

Melt 1 tablespoonful of butter in a frying pan. Put in 6 chops and brown lightly and quickly on both sides. Add 3 carrots cut lengthwise in strips, 6 very small onions, 3 of which should have a dove stuck in, 3 sprigs of parsley, and 1 cup of stock. Let simmer one hour. Serve with any sauce you like, such as sauce piquante, sauce soubise or tomato sauce.

Annette.

FRICANDEAU

Take a nice piece of clearveal, and lard it well. Put into a saucepan 3 carrots cut round, 3 small onions cut in slices. Put your veal upon them and pour in stock until it comes half-way up the meat. Add 1 teaspoonful of salt and a few pepper-corns. When it comes to a boil, put a sheet of buttered paper over it, cover closely, and let it simmer over a low flame for four hours. The fricandeau ought to be a good, brown color. Serve it with sorrel or endive or in its own sauce.

Annette.

VEAL CUTLETS IN PAPERS

Take 2 pounds of veal cutlets, in 2 cutlets and flatten well. Butter a sheet of paper, sprinkle with bread crumbs, mushrooms, and herbs chopped very fine. Salt and pepper. Butter two other sheets of paper and put under the first. Lay your cutlet on, twist your paper round in the form of the piece and tie it with a short piece of thread. Do the same with both cutlets. Put in a baking pan and bake one hour in a moderate oven. When they are done, remove outer paper.

Annette.

ANOTHER WAY

Take 6 lamb chops, put each in sheet of paper that has been well buttered on the inside and dipped in water to prevent burning. Season with salt, pepper and bread crumbs. Roll them in the papers to preserve the gravy, tying the ends of the paper neatly. Bake in a moderate oven three-quarters of an hour. Serve them in the papers.

Volney.

BEEF OLIVES

Take slices of round of beef, cut medium thick, about the size of one's hand. Dip in egg, sprinkle with bread crumbs, salt and pepper, roll them up and tie, or fasten with skewers. Put in a pan and half-cover with stock. Add a little nutmeg and 4 small onions. Stew for one hour, or until tender.

Scotch.

FRENCH BEEFSTEAK

Cut 2 pounds of filet of beef into six pieces. Soak them in olive oil with salt in it for two hours. Put them on the broiler, under a hot flame, and broil ten minutes, turning once. Serve them with a maitre d'hotel sauce and surround with potatoes. The potatoes should be cut in pieces lengthwise, after they have been peeled, and fried in hot butter, turning them all the time that they may be equally brown on all sides.

Annette.

LARDED FILET OF BEEF

Lard 3 pounds of tenderloin of beef. Put it in a deep dish, lay a bay leaf on it along with 3 sprigs of parsley and 3 sliced onions. Pour over it 3/4 cup of olive oil mixed with 3/4 cup of vinegar and let it soak for at least twenty-four hours. Pour the oil and vinegar frequently over the meat, with a spoon, while soaking. When ready to roast, remove from sauce, place on a rack in a roasting pan, sprinkle with salt and pepper and put in bottom of pan 1/4 cupful of suet cut in small pieces. Put in hot oven and bake about thirty minutes. Baste three times during roasting. You may serve it either with or without sauce. If with sauce, you make use of the drippings of the beef to make a sauce piquante.

Annette.

FRENCH ROAST BEEF

Take a rib roast of beef weighing about 6 or 7 pounds and soak it in oil and vinegar as in the preceding recipe, keeping it in half as long again as the tender filet. Put it in a roasting pan, dust with salt, pepper and a little flour, and put in a hot oven. Roast one and a half hours, basting it four or five times. One-half cup of water may be added. Put on a platter and pour the gravy over it, having first skimmed off the grease.

BEEF À LA MODE

Take a pot roast weighing about five pounds and lard it well with bacon that you have first sprinkled with salt, pepper and any desired herbs, chopped fine. Put it in a pan (a Dutch oven is best), add 4 carrots cut in slices lengthwise, 4 small onions, 3 of which must each have a clove stuck in, a knuckle of veal, 4 sprigs of parsley and a cup of stock. Cover and let it cook slowly for four or five hours. The sauce ought to be thick.

Annette.

BEEF À LA MODE

Take 4 pounds of top of the round and cut off most of the fat. Mix together 1 onion chopped fine, 1 sprig of chopped parsley; 1/2 teaspoonful of salt, 1/4 teaspoonful of pepper, 1/8 teaspoonful of grated nutmeg, and 1/4 teaspoonful of thyme. Take 4 strips of lean bacon and the fat from the meat, roll in the above mixture and lard the meat with this. Put 4 pieces of bacon into the bottom of your pan (a Dutch oven is best), lay the beef on it and lay on the roast 4 or 5 more strips of bacon. Cut 3 small onions fine, slice 3 carrots, and put in the pot. Add salt and pepper, 1/4 teaspoonful of grated nutmeg, a pinch of thyme, 1 wineglass of brandy and 1 glass of white wine. Put the pot on a low fire and let boil gently three hours, taking care that the meat does not stick to the bottom. Strain the gravy through a fine sieve, skim off the grease and serve.

Lemaire.

BOUILLI

Take 4 pounds of round of beef, put it in a soup kettle. Pour on 4 quarts of cold water and bring to a boil. Skim the foam as it rises. When the water boils add 1/2 cup cold water to clear it. Skim again. When all scum has been removed set over a very low flame and let it stew gently. Add 2 teaspoonfuls of salt, 8 pepper-corns, 6 whole cloves, 4 onions, 4 carrots, 4 turnips, 1 stalk of celery. When they are tender remove and cut up fine to season the soup.

While the beef is cooking make the glazing as follows: Stew a knuckle of veal with a piece of bacon and the same vegetables and seasoning used in the foregoing. When the meat falls from the bone strain off the broth and simmer until it is of a consistency to coat a spoon when withdrawn from it. Pour this over the boiled beef just before serving. For the gravy, cream 2 tablespoonfuls of butter with 1 of flour, add 1 pickled cucumber, minced, 1 anchovy, crushed, and 1 tablespoon of capers. Put in the same saucepan in which the glazing was prepared. Add 3/4 cupful of water, bring to a boil, stirring constantly. Pour into sauce boat and serve at once.

Lemaire.

BEEF À LA DAUBE

Take 4 pounds of round of beef and lard it well. Put it in a Dutch oven. Cut the meat from a pound of shin of beef and cut in small pieces. Mix with it 1 cupful of veal or lamb, cut in small pieces, and 1/4-pound of bacon cut up. Season the mixture with 1 teaspoonful of salt, 1/2 teaspoonful of pepper, 1/2 teaspoonful of dried thyme or a sprig of fresh, 3 carrots cut in slices and 2 onions, sliced. Put the seasoning around and over the beef. Cover with water. Let cook very slowly until tender. Remove beef and set aside to cool.

The jelly is now to be made. Remove all small pieces of meat, skim the grease off, and pass the gravy through a fine sieve. Put back on the fire and let simmer slowly with a few grains of pepper. Beat the whites of 5 eggs a very little with 1/2 cup of water. Pour into gravy, stir well for five minutes. Bring to a boil, then turn fire low and let simmer twenty minutes. Strain through a fine cheesecloth and you will have a clear jelly. When cool, cut into shapes and garnish the beef with it. This dish should be prepared the day before it is wanted.

Monticello.

TO STEW BEEF

Cut 2 pounds of the top of the round of beef into small cubes. Add 1 pint of white wine, half a grated nutmeg, 4 whole cloves, 8 pepper-corns, 1 teaspoonful of salt, and a slice of ham cut into cubes. Let stew until the meat is tender. Half an hour before serving add 1 stalk of celery cut into fine pieces.

Monticello.

MINCED COLLOPS

Take 2 pounds of any tender cut of cooked beef. Cut into small cubes. Season with 1/2 teaspoonful of grated nutmeg, 1 teaspoonful of salt, 1/2 teaspoonful of pepper. Put into a pan with 1 shredded onion and 3 tablespoonfuls of butter. Turn all over and over until lightly browned. Add 1/2 cup of stock, 1 tablespoonful of catsup, 1 tablespoonful of chopped capers, and 1/2 cupful of sliced mushrooms. Thicken the gravy with 1 tablespoonful of flour mixed with an equal amount of butter. Garnish your dish with forcemeat balls and pickles.

Monticello.

FORCEMEAT

One-half pound of lean bacon, 1/2 pound of suet, chop both fine. Add 1/2 teaspoonful of sweet herbs, shred fine, 1/8 teaspoonful of powdered mace, nutmeg, pepper and salt. Add the yolks of 2 eggs and beat all well together.

Monticello.

BREAST OF MUTTON

Manage it as you did the bouilli. When done season it with salt, pepper and nutmeg to taste. For gravy melt 3 tablespoonfuls of butter, add gradually 2 of grated bread crumbs. Stir until brown. Add 1/4 cupful of the juice of the meat.

Lemaire.

POTTED BEEF

Take 3 pounds of shin of beef. Cut in very small pieces. Put in a pot with the bone, barely cover with water and cook until tender. Set aside to cool. Remove fat. Heat it again, remove bones, and chop meat as fine as for mincemeat. Add to it all the remaining gravy, season to taste with salt, pepper and any desired spices. Turn into moulds.

Mrs. Calver.

STEW MADE OF COLD MEAT

Slice your meat, put it in a pan with 2 large spoonfuls of water, 1/4 teaspoonful of pepper and salt. Just before serving add 3 tablespoonfuls of butter, 2 tablespoonfuls of walnut catsup, 2 of current jelly, 1 teaspoonful of mustard. Let heat thoroughly, and serve.

Edgehill.

BOEUF À LA MODE

Take 4 pounds of round of beef, lard well and season with 1 teaspoonful of salt; 1/2 teaspoonful of pepper, 1 bay leaf. Put it into a pot, brown well, add 1 glass of wine and the juice of a lemon. Let simmer until tender.

Dictionaire de la cuisine.

BOEUF BOUILLI À L'ODDETTE

Melt 3 tablespoonfuls of butter, add 1/2 pound of sliced mushrooms. Sprinkle over all 2 tablespoonfuls of flour and stir well. Pour on 1 1/2 cups of stock, add 1 small onion with a clove stuck in it. Let simmer ten minutes. Add 2 cups of boiled beef cut in small slices. Ladle gravy over all thoroughly. Bring to boiling point. Add the yolk of 1 egg and 1 teaspoonful of vinegar or lemon. Put on a platter. Surround with croutons. Serve.

Baron de Brise.

BEEF OLIVES

Put 1 pound of beef through the food chopper. Add an equal quantity of boiled rice. Season with salt and pepper and stir in 1 egg. Form into small balls and put in a hot oven for twenty minutes.

Septimia Randolph Meikelham's cook, Nancy.

CHICKEN PUDDING No. 1

Disjoint 2 chickens and parboil them. Butter a baking dish and lay the chickens in, dot with butter, season with pepper and salt. Beat 4 eggs until light, add 1 cup of milk, 1 cup of flour, 1 scant teaspoonful baking powder; 1/2 teaspoonful of salt. Pour over the chicken and bake in a moderate oven for one hour.

Mrs. Elizabeth Lea.

CHICKEN PUDDING No. 2

Disjoint 2 young chickens, dust with salt and pepper. Take 1 quart of potatoes, wash and peel them. Cut in slices, boil until tender and mash them. Add 2 tablespoonfuls of butter, salt and pepper to taste, and 1 pint of milk. Put a layer of this in the bottom of a glass baking dish, then a layer of chicken, and so on until the dish is full. Bake one hour in a moderate oven.

COLD FRESH MEAT

Cut any cold, roasted meat in thin slices. Chop fine 2 sprigs of parsley, 1 of thyme, and 3 spears of chives. Mix with 6 tablespoonfuls of bread crumbs, 1/2 teaspoonful of salt, 1/4 teaspoonful of pepper. Sprinkle over the meat, and pour over all 1/2 cup of French dressing.

FILET OF VEAL WITH MADEIRA SAUCE

Take 3 pounds of clear veal, lard with pork, place in a saucepan with 2 tablespoonfuls of butter, 3 carrots cut in slices, 2 sliced onions, a sprig of thyme, 1 bay leaf, and 1 cup of stock. Season with salt and pepper. Cover, and simmer until tender. Serve with a sauce made of the gravy of the meat to which add 1/2 cup of sliced mushrooms, any desired seasoning and 1 wineglass of Madeira wine.

BLANQUETTE OF VEAL

Cut 3 pounds of the breast of veal in pieces 1 inch long. Soak in cold water for two hours. Drain and wipe dry. Melt 4 tablespoonfuls of butter and brown the veal in this. Season with salt and pepper, cover with stock, and stew until tender.

Professor Blot.

BEEFSTEAK PIE

Cut 2 pounds of beefsteak into small pieces. Stew in a little water until half done. Season with salt and pepper. Line a baking dish with puff paste, put in the steak. Season the gravy very high and pour in the dish. Cover with paste and bake until the paste is a nice brown.

Mrs. Mary Randolph.

VEAL CUTLETS

Take 2 pounds of veal cutlets cut in two slices. Lay in a pan with 1/4 pound of pork, a clove of garlic, a sprig of thyme, and 2 of parsley. Cover with water and simmer for fifteen minutes. Remove meat from pan, lay on a dish and let cool. When cold, cover well with sifted bread crumbs mixed with chopped parsley, pepper, salt, and grated nutmeg. Press firmly on veal with a broad knife. When a little dried, turn meat and do the same to other side.

Put 4 tablespoonfuls of lard or other fat in a frying pan. When it starts to smoke drop cutlets in. Brown on both sides. Meanwhile simmer the water in which the veal was cooked until it is reduced to one cupful. Strain it and thicken with 1 tablespoonful of butter mixed with 1 tablespoonful of flour. Add 1/2 cup of wine, 1/4 cup of mushroom catsup, put in the cutlets and stew until tender. Serve with forcemeat balls.

Mrs. Mary Randolph.

PIE OF SWEETBREADS AND OYSTERS

Drop a sweetbread into acidulated salted boiling water and cook slowly for twenty minutes. Plunge into cold water. Drain and cut in cubes. Stew a pint of oysters until the edges curl. Add 2 tablespoonfuls of butter creamed with 1 tablespoonful of flour, 1 cup of cream and the yolks of 3 eggs well beaten. Season with salt and pepper to taste. Line a deep baking dish with puff paste. Put in a layer of oysters, then a layer of sweetbreads until the dish is nearly full. Pour the sauce over all and put a crust on top. Bake until the paste is a delicate brown. This is the most delicate pie that can be made.

BOILED LEG OF MUTTON

Dredge a leg of mutton with flour and put in a kettle. Cover with cold water. Add 2 teaspoonfuls of salt, 1 small garlic, which will give it a delicately fine flavor. Bring to a boil. Skim well. When tender remove from broth and cover to keep hot. Have ready 6 carrots cut in slices and cooked, 4 turnips boiled and mashed with a lump of butter. Salt and pepper. Lay the mutton on this. Melt 4 tablespoonfuls of butter, add 1 tablespoonful of flour, 4 tablespoonfuls of capers with some of the vinegar in which they came. Mix all well together and spread over the mutton.

Mrs. Mary Randolph.

HARICOT OF MUTTON

Take a rack of mutton, separate into chops, beat flat, sprinkle with salt and pepper and broil until a pale brown. Stew the trimmings with 2 cups of water, strain, season well with salt, pepper, a pinch of thyme, and any preferred catsup. Simmer until reduced by one-half. Thicken with 1 tablespoonful of butter rolled in flour. Have ready 4 carrots and 2 turnips cut into small dice and boiled until tender. Put in the gravy, heat all well, and serve.

Mrs. Mary Randolph.

MUTTON CHOPS

Cut a rack of mutton as for haricot. Stew in 2 cups of water, 1 teaspoonful of salt, 1/4 teaspoonful of pepper, until tender. Prepare a gravy with 1 table-spoonful of butter, 2 tablespoonfuls boiling water, 1 tablespoonful of mushroom catsup, 1/2 teaspoonful of salt. Stir thoroughly and pour over the meat.

Mrs. Mary Randolph.

TO BOIL A HAM

Ham should be washed and soaked all night in cold water. The next morning scrape and wash well, put on to boil in water to cover it more than well. Boil for five, six, or even seven hours. It is not done until the bone in the under part comes off with ease. But it is best not to boil it until the meat is in strings.

Monticello.

Hams improve in flavor until they are two years old. After that they are neither better or worse.

Monticello.

HAM WITH BREAD CRUMBS

This is always done in the hams of the first year. Boil as in preceding receipt and remove the skin. Cover the top slightly with bread crumbs and put in the oven until of a light brown.

Monticello.

GLAZED HAM

Take the skin off of the boiled ham—old ham—and let it get cold. Sprinkle it thick with sugar. Set under a broiler and glaze it well.

Monticallo.

BOILED TURKEY WITH OYSTER SAUCE

Grate a loaf of bread, chop a dozen large oysters fine, add 1/4 teaspoonful of nutmeg, 1/2 teaspoonful of salt, 1/2 teaspoonful of pepper. Mix into a light forcemeat with 1/4 pound of butter, 2 tablespoonfuls of cream and 3 eggs. Stuff the turkey, making any remaining into balls and boil them. Sew up the turkey, dredge with flour, and put in a kettle with enough cold water to cover well. Set over a medium fire. As the scum begins to rise, remove it. Let it boil very slowly one hour. Remove kettle from heat and keep closely covered another hour. The steam being kept in will stew it enough, make it rise, keep the skin whole, tender and very white. When you serve it, pour on a little oyster sauce, lay the balls around and serve the rest of the sauce in a boat. Put it on the fire to heat just before serving.

Mrs. Mary Randolph.

SAUCE FOR THE TURKEY

Drain 1 pint of oysters. Add the juice to 1 cupful of cream sauce. Add 1 teaspoonful of lemon pickle, 1 tablespoonful of butter mixed with 1 tablespoonful of flour and 1 tablespoonful of cream. Add the oysters and stir until they are hot, but do not boil for it will make them hard and appear small.

Mrs. Mary Randolph.

TURKEY À LA DAUBE

Bone a small turkey. Put pepper and salt on the inside and cover with slices of ham or boiled tongue. Fill it with a seasoned forcemeat. Sew it up and boil gently until tender. Cover it with jelly and serve.

Mrs. Mary Randolph.

ROASTED GOOSE

Chop a few sage leaves and 2 onions very fine, mix with 2 tablespoonfuls of butter, 1 teaspoonful of pepper, 2 teaspoonfuls of salt. Put it in the goose. Rub over with butter, dredge with flour, and put in a hot oven. Baste with melted butter. Roast one and one-half hours. Add 1/2 cup boiling water to the gravy.

Mrs. Mary Randolph.

SAUCE FOR A GOOSE

Pare, core and slice 6 apples. Put them in a saucepan with just enough water to prevent them from sticking. Set over a very slow fire and cook until reduced to a pulp. Add 1 tablespoonful of butter, sugar to taste and beat well.

Mrs. Mary Randolph.

ROASTED DUCKS

Shred 1 onion and a few sage leaves fine. Put them in the duck with 1/2 teaspoonful of salt and 1/2 teaspoonful of pepper. Dust with flour and put in a hot oven. Baste with melted butter. If your oven is very hot it will roast in half an hour. The quicker it is roasted the better it will taste. Prepare a gravy with the broth from the gizzard, liver and heart which have been stewed. Into the broth put a large blade of mace, four pepper-corns, 1 tablespoonful of catsup, 1 teaspoonful of lemon pickle. Strain and pour it on the ducks. Serve onion sauce in a boat.

Mrs. Mary Randolph.

ROASTED WILD DUCKS OR TEAL

Put into each of your ducks a small onion, 1/2 teaspoonful of salt, 1/4 teaspoonful of pepper and 1 tablespoonful of red wine. Put in a very hot oven and roast twenty minutes. Make a gravy of the necks and gizzards, 1 tablespoonful of red wine, half an anchovy, a blade of mace, 1 onion, salt and a dash of cayenne pepper. Cook in 2 cups of water and simmer until reduced to 1 cup. Strain through a fine sieve and pour over the ducks. Serve with onion sauce in a boat.

Mrs. Mary Randolph.

CHICKEN PIE

Boil 2 young chickens in salted water barely to cover them for one-half hour. Have a sprig of parsley, a few celery leaves and 2 whole cloves in the water. Cut them in small pieces, removing all skin. Have a deep dish lined with pastry, already baked. Put in a layer of chicken, sprinkle with flour, salt, pepper, a little mace and some of the chopped hearts and livers. Continue until dish is full. Pour in as much of the liquor in which the chickens were cooked as the dish will hold. Wet the edges of the pastry with water, lay on the top crust, close the edges carefully, prick well, and bake until the top crust is done. The crust for a chicken pie should be thicker than for a fruit pie.

Mrs. Horace Mann.

FRIED CHICKEN

Disjoint 2 young chickens. Dredge the pieces well with flour, sprinkle with salt and pepper and drop into deep fat. Fry until a golden brown. Brown small circles of cold mush (cornmeal boiled in water with salt and poured in a pan until cold), and fry a dozen sprigs of parsley, to garnish the dish. Scald 1 cup of cream, add 1 tablespoonful of butter, salt and pepper to taste, and 1 teaspoonful of chopped parsley. Pour over the chickens and serve.

Mrs. Mary Randolph.

VENISON

Lard well a saddle of venison, dust with salt and pepper. Put in a hot oven. Baste with cream, as it is not very fat. Serve with currant jelly sauce.

Mrs. Horace Mann.

FISH

HOW TO ASCERTAIN IF FISH, WHETHER BOILED, STEWED, OR FRIED, IS DONE

If the bone sticks firm to the flesh, or the flesh to the bone, it is not done. By the same rule, if quite loose, and the flesh of the fish drops off the bone, it is overdone, and you lose some of its qualities. For fish in slices, try the bone with your knife; if the flesh comes from it, it is done; or by placing the point of a knife between the flesh and the bone, and on raising it, if done, the knife will part it easily.

To boil a large fish whole it is requisite to have a drain at the bottom of the kettle.

Soyer.

NEW WAY OF BOILING FISH

The addition of a few herbs and vegetables in the water gives a very nice flavor to the fish. Add, according to taste, half a sliced onion, a sprig of thyme, a bay leaf, winter savory, 2 carrots, a stalk of celery, 3 or 4 whole cloves, a blade of mace, using whichever of the ingredients you have at hand.

Fresh water fish, which have no particular flavor, are preferable done thus, with the addition of a little vinegar.

Soyer.

BAKED FISH

Wash well a sole, or other fish, and dry thoroughly. Chop fine 1 onion and 4 or 5 sprigs of parsley. Put 2 tablespoonfuls of melted butter in your baking pan.

Sprinkle some of the chopped onion and parsley on it and lay the fish on this. Season with salt and pepper. Mix the remainder of the chopped onion and parsley with bread crumbs, about 3/4 cup more or less according to size of fish. Dot over with butter and pour a glass of wine or broth in the pan. Bake until done. A large sole will require about an hour. If necessary, put under the broiler a few moments to brown nicely.

Soyer.

REMAINS OF BOILED FISH

The remains of boiled fish may always be prepared as above. A few spoonfuls of melted butter poured over the fish before strewing on the crumbs makes it more delicate.

Soyer.

TO DRESS CODFISH No. 1

Boil your fish in salted water until tender. Scald 1 cup of milk and 1 cup of cream with 2 tablespoonfuls of butter. Shred your fish fine and put it in this gravy. Simmer for fifteen minutes. Add 4 hard-boiled eggs chopped fine and a good dash of nutmeg. Put on a platter, cover with the yolks of 2 hard-boiled eggs pressed through a sieve, and serve.

Monticello.

FISH WITH POTATOES

Boil and shred your fish. Have ready same mashed potatoes. Mix them, in equal quantities, with 2 table-spoonfuls of butter, 1/4 teaspoonful of grated nutmeg, 1/8 teaspoonful of pepper, 1/2 teaspoonful of salt, and 2 tablespoonfuls of brandy. Beat well. If too stiff, add more cream or milk. Turn into a dish lined with pie crust and bake until set.

Martha Jefferson Randolph.

TO FRY FISH

The great art in frying fish is to have it free from grease. It is important to have plenty of fat in the pan and to have it very hot. If at the proper degree of temperature, a sole and an apple fritter may be fried in the same pan, without either tasting of the other. To ascertain the proper degree of heat put a cube of bread in the fat. If it hisses, the fat is ready. If the bread burns, it is too hot. If the bread is a delicate brown, the fat is just right. The fish should be dipped in egg, then in bread crumbs with which salt and pepper have been mixed. Shake off all loose crumbs before putting in pan. Turn once while frying.

Soyer.

OYSTER PIE

Line a dish with pastry and bake it. Take 1 quart of oysters, put the juice in a saucepan with 1/2 teaspoonful of mace, a glass of wine, the juice of 1 lemon, and bring to a boil. Pour in 1 cup of cream and thicken the gravy with 2 scant tablespoonfuls of flour mixed with 2 tablespoonfuls of butter. Add the oysters and bring to a boil. Pour into the prepared crust. The upper crust should have been baked separately on a baking sheet and laid on top of the pie after the oysters are put in.

Mrs. Horace Mann.

TONGUES AND SOUNDS

The principal thing to be observed in dressing tongues and sounds is to freshen them as much as possible by washing and soaking. When all possible salt has been removed they should be boiled until thoroughly done. They may be served plain or with any desired sauce, or they may be mixed with enough melted butter, pepper, and chopped parsley to form a sauce for them.

BROILED SHAD

Separate one side from the backbone so that it will lie open without being split in two. Wash thoroughly, dry with a clean cloth and sprinkle with salt and pepper. Let it stand until you are ready to broil it. Put under a hot broiler, broil until a nice brown. Pour melted butter over it and serve.

Mrs. Mary Randolph.

FRIED FISH, JEWISH FASHION

Take a pound piece of halibut, lay in a dish. Sprinkle salt on the top and put some water in the dish, about half way up the fish. Let stand one hour. Take it out, dry it, cut out the bones. It is then in two pieces. Lay the pieces on their side and cut in slices one-half inch thick. Put 1/4 pound of any desired fat in a frying pan. Mix 4 tablespoonfuls of flour with 1 egg and a little water to form a smooth batter, not too thick. Dip the fish in this, until well covered, drop in the hot fat and fry to a golden brown.

Drain in brown paper, put on platter and serve. Any desired sauce may be used, but plain, with salt and lemon is usual. Other fish may be done in this way.

Soyer.

BOILED ROCKFISH

The best part of the rock is the head and shoulders. Put it into a fish kettle with enough water to cover and 1 teaspoonful of salt. Boil gently and skim well. When tender drain off the water and lay the fish on a platter. Garnish with grated horseradish. Serve with melted butter mixed with chopped parsley or, for a change, with anchovy butter. The roe and liver should be fried and served separately.

Mrs. Mary Randolph.

FRIED PERCH

Clean the fish well but do not remove the roes. Dry, sprinkle with salt and pepper and dredge with flour. Lay them on a board. When one side is dry, turn, sprinkle other side with salt, pepper and flour. Drop into hot fat and fry until a golden brown. It takes about five minutes. Serve with melted butter or anchovy sauce.

Mrs. Mary Randolph.

VEGETABLES

DRESSING VEGETABLES

Lard is even better than butter for frying vegetables, but must be kept at a high temperature or the vegetables will taste of it.

SALSIFY

Salsify must be scraped and not prepared until it is time to cook it or it will turn dark.

One way to dress salsify is to boil it after it is scraped. When tender, mash and fry in little cakes the size of sausages. Another way is to scrape and cut in small pieces the size of dice. Boil until tender. Put in a pan with a lump of butter, a little milk, flour, or bread crumbs, pepper and salt, and stew for twenty minutes.

Third way for salsify. Scrape, cut it lengthwise, and fry it.

TURNIPS

Peel and boil until tender as many turnips as desired. Mash through a colander. Add butter, salt, pepper and a little milk, and stew for fifteen minutes so as to dry them.

With sugar. Peel turnips, cut in pieces and put them in a vessel with a spoonful of butter, half a cup of brown sugar and a pint of hot water. Stew until tender.

At Monticello we used to have turnips dressed with cheese.

POLENTA

Make mush (corn meal boiled in salt water, slowly, until thick) and turn into a square pan. When cold, cut in thin slices and lay in a baking dish, grate cheese over the mush, and dot with butter. Repeat these layers, letting a layer of cheese and butter be on top, until the dish is full. Bake in a moderate oven until the cheese is thoroughly melted.

MACARONI

Break macaroni in small pieces, there should be 2 cupfuls, and boil in salted water until tender. Grate 1/4 pound of cheese and mix with the same amount of butter. Stir into the macaroni and bake like polenta.

POTATOES

Potatoes may be wrung in a cloth after they are boiled. This is good when they are small or indifferent. When they are small, several can be wrung together.

They may be mashed, with milk and butter added after they are boiled. Serve them thus, or form into cakes, and fried like salsify.

CARTHUSIAN

Cut a head of Savoy cabbage in 4 pieces, wash well. Put in an iron pot with 3 quarts of water and boil for fifteen minutes. Drain in a colander and press out all the water. Remove the stalk from each piece and chop, not too fine. The monks always had a foundation of cabbage, or of greens, or of Brussels sprouts, one pound of either, prepared as above. Then they added 1 pound either of boiled carrots, turnips, parsnips, beets, artichokes, potatoes, leeks, celery or onions. Boil the pound of whatever you choose from the above until tender. Chop it as you did the cabbage, adding 1/2 teaspoonful of salt. Take 3 medium-sized pig's tongues, which should have been boiled with the cabbage, cut them through lengthwise. Line your pan on the bottom and around the sides with the chopped vegetables, about an inch deep. Place the meat in the center, thus making it invisible when turned out. When filled add 1/4 pound of butter, 1 wineglassful of vinegar, and 1/2 cup of water. Cover and set upon a very slow fire for two hours. Then drain all the gravy into a bowl. Run a knife around the pot, put platter over the pan, reverse, turn out, and your Carthusian will appear as a pudding. Pour the gravy, or bread-crumb sauce over it and serve.

You may also, for a change, pour a little white or brown sauce over it, but take care that the vegetables must always be kept firm enough to turn out like a pudding.

Soyer.

PARSNIPS
Parsnips; may be cooked, mashed and fried in cakes like salsify.

FOR VEGETARIANS
The foregoing will, by omitting the meat, be applicable to vegetarians.

HOW IT MAY BE VARIED

Instead of tongue you may use pigs' feet, pickled pork, bacon, ham, liver of all kinds, previously fried, or partly so; sausages, salt beef, previously boiled and cut in slices, or any part of fresh meats previously roasted and cut in slices. Pigeons or partridges and all kinds of small birds may be put in rows, only they should be larded and stuffed previously.

Soyer.

CHARTREUSE

At Monticello the vegetables, all roots, no cabbage, were cut in slices and arranged in a fanciful way, alternating carrots with white vegetables, in a mould with straight sides. The mould was filled with forced meat balls. It turned out in a beautiful form and made a very pretty dish for a ceremonious dinner.

Monticello.

PODRILLA LÀ CREOLE

Put 1 pint of red beans to soak the night before. Drain in the morning. Cover with water, and set on the fire. Add 1/4 pound salt pork cut into cubes. Season with salt and pepper to taste, add a bunch of herbs, bring to a boil and let cook very slowly until tender.

Wash 1 cup of rice well and boil in salted water until light and tender. Add 2 tablespoonfuls of butter, salt and pepper to taste. Press into a ring mould set in a moderate oven for ten minutes. Turn out and fill the center with the beans which have been drained and from which the herbs have been removed.

Baron de Brise.

PUDDINGS

SOUTH CAROLINA RICE PUDDING

Beat the yolks of 5 eggs, add gradually 4 table-spoonfuls of sugar, and 1 pint of milk. Beat the whites of the eggs until stiff and mix with the yolks. Stir 2 tablespoonfuls of melted butter into 3/4 cup of rice. Put into a baking dish and add about half the egg, a pinch of salt and milk mixture. Stir well. Pour the rest of the first mixture over it, add a piece of stick cinnamon, and bake in a moderate oven until set.

Mrs. Allston.

GÂTEAU AU RIZ

Wash 6 tablespoonfuls of rice in several waters. Put in a saucepan and pour on 4 cups of milk. Cook until the rice is puffed and tender. Sweeten to taste and set aside to cool. When quite cold add the yolks of 4 eggs, and the grated rind of 1/2 lemon. Beat the whites to a froth and add to the rice. Butter a mould and dust with bread crumbs. Pour the rice mixture into the mould, set in a pan of water and bake one-half hour. Serve with the following sauce.

Annette.

SAUCE FOR ABOVE

Bring 1 1/2 cups of milk to a boil. Beat the yolks of 2 eggs until light, add 3 tablespoonfuls of sugar, 1/2 tablespoonful of flour, a pinch of salt. Simmer, stirring constantly, until slightly thick. Strain, let cool, add 1/2 teaspoonful of vanilla extract.

Annette.

PHILADELPHIA PUDDING

Wash 1 teaspoonful of rice well and stir it into 3 pints of milk. Sweeten to taste, add pinch of salt, and flavor with nutmeg, vanilla, or cinnamon. When all is mixed set over a very low flame for five or six hours. It must not be stirred or put over too hot a fire.

Virginia Randolph Trist,

INDIAN PUDDING No. 1

Chop fine 1/2 pound of suet. Mix with 1/2 cup of corn meal, 1 cup of molasses, 1/4 teaspoonful of salt, and 1 quart of milk. Stir well and pour into baking dish. Set in a slow oven. As it bakes, add more milk to prevent it thickening and hardening. Two hours will bake it. It is eaten with butter and sugar, or molasses.

Boston.

INDIAN MEAL PUDDING No. 2

Mix 8 tablespoonfuls of meal with 1 cup of molasses, add 2 tablespoonfuls of melted butter, and 1/4 teaspoonful of salt. Beat 2 eggs light and stir in first mixture. Add slowly 1 quart of milk that has been brought to a boil. Bake for two hours in a slow oven.

BOILED LOAF

Cut the crust off a loaf of bread and put it in a deep dish. Pour 1 cupful of milk over it and let it soak thoroughly. Then boil it in water to cover, but not long enough for it to fall to pieces. It should preserve the form of the loaf. Serve with any preferred sauce.

Monticello.

BREAD PUDDING No. 1

Cut the crusts off a loaf of bread and slice the bread into a deep dish. Pour 1 quart of scalded milk over it and let it soak an hour. Stir until the lumps are all dissolved. Beat 5 eggs until very light. Add to first mixture, with 1/2 cup of sugar and 1/4 teaspoonful of salt. Take a square pudding cloth, dip in cold water, wring out and dust well with flour. Pour the pudding into this, tie tightly, and boil for two hours.

Ellen Randolph Coolidge.

SAUCE FOR THE ABOVE

Mix 1 cup of sugar with 1 tablespoonful of flour and a pinch of salt. Add the juice and rind of 1 lemon and 1 cup of boiling water. Add 2 tablespoonfuls of butter, simmer for five minutes, strain and serve.

Ellen Randolph Coolidge.

BREAD PUDDING No. 2

Remove the crusts from a loaf of bread and crumble the bread fine. Add it to a quart of milk, bring to a boil and let simmer for fifteen minutes. Beat the yolks of 6 eggs and the whites of 3 until light. Add 6 table-spoonfuls of sugar, 1/4 teaspoonful of salt and the grated rind of 1 lemon. Beat all well together and bake in a moderate oven for three-quarters of an hour.

SAUCE

Melt 2 tablespoonfuls of butter, add 2 of brandy, 1 cupful of sugar mixed with 1 teaspoonful of flour. Stir over a slow fire until it thickens.

Martha Jefferson Randolph,

BREAD AND BUTTER PUDDING

Cut a stale, square loaf of bread in slices and spread each slice with a thick layer of butter. Take a deep baking dish, cover the bottom with bread, strew in a few currants or stoned raisins, then another layer of bread, and so on until the dish is two-thirds full. Beat 6 eggs, add 1 cupful of sugar, 4 cups of milk, and any kind of seasoning that is preferred. Pour this into the dish and let stand two hours. Bake one and one-half hours in a slow oven.

Mrs. Putnam.

BATTER PUDDING No. 1

Mix 3 tablespoonfuls of flour with 1/4 teaspoonful of salt and a little grated nutmeg. Stir into this 2 cups of milk and cook until it thickens. Add 4 tablespoonfuls of butter and let cool. When cold, add 6 well-beaten eggs. Beat all together thoroughly. Butter a mould, pour in the pudding, cover, and boil for two and one-half hours. Serve with wine sauce.

BATTER PUDDING No. 2

Beat 6 eggs, and 4 cups milk, 1/4 teaspoonful of salt and enough flour to make a thin batter. Grease a baking dish well, pour your pudding in and bake in a very hot oven. One-half hour should bake it.

Harriet Douglas.

CORN PUDDING

Grate 6 ears of green corn. Mix with it 1/2 cup of cream, a tablespoonful of butter, 1/2 tablespoonful of sugar and a sprinkle of salt. Mix all well together and bake.

Mrs. Derby, Newport.

GÂTEAU DE POMME DE TERRE

Peel 6 large potatoes, cut them up and place in a saucepan. Cover with water and boil until tender. Drain and press them through a colander. Add the well-beaten yolks of 3 eggs, and sugar to taste. Beat the whites of the eggs to a stiff froth and fold them into the first mixture. Butter a mould well and dust with bread crumbs. Pour in the pudding and bake in a moderate oven until set, from one-half to three-quarters of an hour.

Annette.

LAID PUDDING

Remove the crusts from a loaf of bread, slice the bread and lay to soak in 2 cups of scalded milk. Put a layer of the bread in a baking dish, sprinkle with a layer of currants. Alternate bread and currants until the dish is nearly full. Pour in 2 cups of milk and 2 cups of cream, mixed and sweetened to taste. Add 1/4 cup of brandy, 1/4 cup of wine, 1/2 cup of almonds blanched and chopped fine, and 1 table-spoonful of candied orange or lemon peel, finely chopped, also 1/8 teaspoonful of nutmeg, of cloves and of mace. Bake the pudding in a moderate oven until set. Serve with melted butter, wine and sugar.

English.

PROPORTIONS OF A PLUM PUDDING

Mix together 1 pound of chopped suet, 4 table-spoonfuls of brown sugar, 1/2 pound of currants, 1 pound of raisins, 3 tablespoonfuls of flour, 4 cups of grated bread crumbs, 12 eggs, 1 grated nutmeg, 1 teaspoonful of cinnamon, 1 of mace, 1 tablespoonful of finely cut citron, 1 teaspoonful of salt, and 1 wineglass of brandy.

WYETH'S ENGLISH PLUM PUDDING

Two pounds of best seedless raisins, 1 pound currants, 1 pound sultana raisins, 1 quart grated bread crumbs, 1 quart beef suet chopped fine, 1/2 pound citron cut fine, 2 ounces candied orange peel, 2 ounces candied lemon peel cut fine, 1 grated nutmeg, 1 teaspoonful of ginger, 1 of salt. Mix all well together. Beat 12 eggs and stir into the first mixture. Add 1 cup of brandy. If not moist enough add as much milk as will make it cling together. Put into tin forms and boil four or five hours. The water must be boiling when the pudding is put in. Plunge into cold water for a few minutes before turning out the pudding.

PLAIN PLUM PUDDING

Chop fine 1 cup of suet, mix in 1 1/2 cups of sugar, 3 cups flour, 1/2 cup molasses, 2 cups raisins, 1 cup currants, 1 teaspoonful of soda dissolved in 1 table-spoonful of hot water and added to 1 cup of milk. Dip a cloth in boiling water, dredge it with flour, tie the pudding in it. Drop in boiling water and boil for two and one-half hours. Serve with any desired warm sauce.

Sarah Buckley.

CHEESE CURD PUDDING

Mix 2 quarts of milk with 1 pint of white wine and heat. Drain all the curd from the whey. Put it in a bowl with 1/2 cup unsalted butter and beat curd and butter together until well mixed. Beat the yolks of 3 eggs and the whites of 2 and add to the curd. Stir in 1/2 cup of fine cake crumbs. Sweeten to taste and add a pinch of salt. Butter a baking dish and turn mixture into it. Bake in a slow oven until set. Serve with melted butter, wine and sugar.

Martha Jefferson Randolph.

APPLE PUDDING

Peel and boil until tender 3 or 4 apples. Press through a sieve. To 1 cup of the purée add 1/2 cup of cream and butter. Let cool. Add 3 well-beaten eggs, 1/2 cup of powdered sugar, the rind of 1 lemon. Mix all well together and put in a crust. Half an hour will bake it.

Monticello.

This pudding is made with either fresh or dried apples.

CURATE PUDDING

Four eggs, their weight in flour, the weight of 3 eggs in sugar. Cream the butter, add sugar gradually and stir untill a smooth paste. Separate the eggs. Mix the yolks with the sugar and butter, then add flour, and stifly beaten egg whites, alternately, along with a pinch of salt. Put in a mould, tie a cloth over top of mould and set in a pan of boiling water. Let the water come half-way up the mould. Renew as it boils away. Steam for two hours.

Mrs. Cox, Manhasset.

LEMON PUDDING No. 1

Beat the yolks of 4 eggs until very light. Cream 1/4 cup of butter with 1 cup of sugar. Stir the yolks into this very gradually. Add the juice of 3 lemons and the grated rind of 1; also a pinch of salt. Put in a double boiler and cook until it thickens, stirring constantly. Have ready muffin pans lined with pastry. Pour the lemon mixture into them and bake in a moderate oven until done. Try with a straw; if the straw comes out clean, it is done.

Martha Jefferson Randolph.

LEMON PUDDING No. 2

Cream 1 cup of butter with 1 cup of sugar. Beat the yolks of 6 eggs until light. Add the juice and grated rind of 2 lemons. Combine mixtures and beat together until very light, add a pinch of salt. Pour into a baking dish lined with puff paste and bake three-quarters of an hour in a moderate oven.

If the butter and sugar are melted together and the

eggs added while warm, it will make a transparent pudding.

Philadelphia.

LEMON PUDDING No. 3

Beat 6 eggs until very light. Add 1 1/2 cups of sugar, 1/4 cup melted butter, the juice and rind of 2 lemons, and a pinch of salt. Pour into a baking pan lined with pastry and bake until set.

Mrs. Fairfax.

MOLASSES AND BREAD PUDDING

Cut slices of bread, butter them well and lay in a pudding dish. Pour a layer of molasses over them. Do this until your dish is full. Set in a *very slow* oven and let it cook gradually for an hour or more. Set under broiler to brown before serving.

Mrs. Beverly Randolph.

APPLE PUDDING

Pare and chop 8 apples. Butter a pudding dish and dust with bread crumbs and a layer of brown sugar. Add a layer of the apples, dot over with 1 tablespoonful of chopped citron and spices to taste. Repeat the crumbs, sugar, apples, spices and citron until your dish is full. Dot over with butter and bake one hour in a moderate oven.

Miss Martin.

SAGO PUDDING No. 1

Scald 3 cups of milk with a piece of stick cinnamon, a piece of lemon rind and a dash of nutmeg. Add 3 tablespoonfuls of sago and cook until clear. Beat 4 eggs with 6 tablespoonfuls of sugar and a pinch of salt, add to first mixture. Remove cinnamon and lemon peel. Pour into a dish lined with pastry and bake until set.

Domestic Cookery.

SAGO PUDDING No. 2

Scald 4 cups of milk with a piece of stick cinnamon. Add 8 tablespoonfuls of sago. Stir often. When thick, remove cinnamon; add 1 cup of butter, 1 cup of sugar, 1/2 cup of wine, and a pinch of salt. When cold add 6 well-beaten eggs and 1/2 cup of currants that have been soaked in hot water. Turn into a baking pan lined with pastry and bake until set.

Mrs. Mary Randolph.

ALMOND PUDDING

Put 1/2 pound of blanched almonds through the food chopper, using finest grinder. Warm slightly 2 tablespoonfuls of cream and add 1/2 cup of butter. When melted stir into the almonds. Add 1 table-spoonful of brandy, a pinch of salt, a dash of nutmeg and sugar to taste. Butter custard cups, fill half full, set in a pan of water and bake until set. Serve with butter, wine and sugar.

Domestic Cookery.

BREAD AND BUTTER PUDDING No. 2

Slice some bread, spread well with butter and lay in a baking dish with currants and sliced citron and lemon or orange peel between each layer of bread.

Pour over this an unboiled custard made by beating 3 eggs, adding 2 cups of milk, 3 tablespoonfuls of sugar, a pinch of salt. Let stand two hours. Bake in a slow oven one hour.

A rim of pastry around the edge makes all puddings look better, but is not necessary.

Domestic Cookery.

ORANGE PUDDING

Cream 3/4 cup butter, add the grated rind of 1 orange and 1 cup of sugar. Beat until very light. Add 6 eggs well beaten. Grate a raw apple and add to first mixture. Line the bottom and sides of a pie plate with pastry. Pour in the orange mixture and over it put cross-bars of pastry. Bake half an hour.

Domestic Cookery.

BROWN BREAD PUDDING

One-half pound of brown bread, grated, 1/2 pound of currants, 1/2 pound of chopped suet. Add 1 cup of sugar and 1/2 grated nutmeg. Mix in 4 well-beaten eggs, 1 tablespoonful of brandy and 2 tablespoonfuls of cream. Pour into a well-buttered mould, or a pudding cloth, and boil from three to four hours.

Domestic Cookery.

TAPIOCA PUDDING

Add 1 cup of tapioca to 2 cups of milk and set over a very slow fire to swell. Stir often. Add 1 pint of cold milk, the yolks of 4 eggs, 1 1/2 cups of sugar, spice, or flavoring to suit taste, 1 cup of currants and 1 cup of raisins. Bake one hour in a slow oven.

Mrs. Putnam.

SWEET POTATO PUDDING No. 1

Boil 1 pound of sweet potatoes until tender. Rub them through a sieve. Add 5 well-beaten eggs, 1 1/2 cups of sugar, 1 cup of butter, the grated rind of 1 lemon, a dash of nutmeg, and a wineglass of brandy. Line a baking dish with pastry and pour in the mixture. Sprinkle with sugar and bits of citron and bake in a slow oven until set.

Mrs. Mary Randolph.

TANSY PUDDING

Beat 6 eggs until light. Add 1 pint of cream, 1 cup of spinach juice, 1/4 cup of juice of tansy. Add 1 cup of sifted cracker crumbs, 1 wineglass of wine, a dash of grated nutmeg, a pinch of salt, and sugar to taste. Stir over a low flame until it thickens. Pour into a baking dish lined with pastry and bake until set. It may be fried like an omelette.

Mrs. Mary Randolph.

GROUND RICE PUDDING

Mix 3 tablespoonfuls of ground rice with 1/2 cup of cold milk. Stir it into 4 cups of scalding milk. Let it simmer for twenty minutes, stirring constantly. When cold, add 4 eggs, the juice of 1 lemon, and sugar to taste. Bake one hour. Line the dish with pastry, or not.

Mrs. Putnam.

ARROWROOT PUDDING

Mix 1 tablespoonful of arrowroot with 2 tablespoonfuls of cold milk. Pour into 2 cups of boiling milk. Add 2/3 cup of sugar and stir constantly. Add a dash of mace or any other flavoring, and 4 well-beaten eggs. Pour into a baking dish lined with pastry and bake until set. If it is preferred to look clear, substitute water for milk and add one more egg.

Mrs. Putnam.

PINEAPPLE PUDDING

Peel the pineapple, taking care to get all the specks out, and grate it. Take its weight in sugar and half its weight in butter. Rub the butter and sugar to a cream and stir them into the pineapple. Add 5 well-beaten eggs and 1 cup of cream. It may be baked with or without the pastry crust.

Mrs. Putnam.

COLD SAUCE

Cream 1 cup of butter. Add 1/2 cup of sugar and stir well until very light. Add the juice and grated rind of 1 lemon, and any additional flavor desired.

Mrs. Putnam.

GRATED APPLE PUDDING

Pare 8 apples and put in water. Cream 1/2 cup butter, add 3/4 cup sugar and mix well. Stir in the juice and rind of 1 lemon. Grate the apples into this mixture. Add 5 wellbeaten eggs and 1 cup of milk. Bake with or without a puff paste lining the dish.

Annette.

PLAIN LEMON PUDDING

Mix juice and grated rind of 2 lemons with 2 cups of water and 2 cups of sugar. Add 2 well-beaten eggs, a pinch of salt, and 6 soda crackers., rolled to fine crumbs. Turn into dish and bake until set.

A GOOD PUDDING

Line a baking dish with slices of bread that have been dipped in milk. Fill the dish with sliced apples, mixed with sugar and spice to taste. Cover with slices of bread soaked in milk. Set a cover on dish and bake one and one-half hours in a slow oven.

TAPIOCA PUDDING

Put a cupful of tapioca and 1/2 teaspoonful of salt into 1 pint of water and let stand overnight. Peel 6 apples, core, and put in a pudding dish. Fill the centers with sugar mixed with a little nutmeg or lemon peel. Add 1 cup of water and bake one hour, turning to prevent drying. When the apples are quite soft pour over them the tapioca and bake one hour. Serve with hard sauce and cream.

DELMONICO PUDDING

Mix 3 tablespoonfuls of cornstarch with a little cold milk. Stir into 1 quart of hot milk, bring to a boil, and boil over a low fire for three minutes. Separate 5 eggs. Beat the yolks with 6 tablespoonfuls of sugar. Pour first mixture into this and bring to a boil. Flavor with vanilla, a pinch of salt, and strain into a pudding dish. Bake until firm. Beat the whites of the eggs to a stiff froth. Add gradually 3 tablespoonfuls of sugar and 1/2 teaspoonful of lemon juice. Drop into the custard from the end of a spoon, in the shape of kisses. Put in the oven until light brown. Serve cold.

A PLAIN PUDDING

Peel 6 tart apples and grate them into a dish. Add an equal quantity of stale bread, grated. Beat 2 eggs, add 2 cups milk and 3 tablespoonfuls of sugar, dash of salt, and flavor with grated lemon or orange peel. Pour on the first mixture, stir well, and bake until set.

Annette.

FRUIT PUDDING

Mix 1 cup of seeded raisins, 1 cup of currants, 1 cup of chopped suet, 1 cup sour milk, 1 teaspoonful of soda dissolved in 1 tablespoonful of hot water, 1/2 cup of molasses, 3 cups of flour, mixed with 1 teaspoonful of allspice, 1 of cloves, 1 of salt. Turn into a mould and boil three hours.

A VERY NICE SAUCE

Cream 1/2 cup of butter with 1 cup of powdered sugar. Beat until light. Add 1 wineglass of hot wine with a dash of nutmeg. Serve at once.

Mrs. Annie Trist.

A SIMPLE BATTER PUDDING

To 1 quart of boiling milk add 4 tablespoonfuls of Indian (corn) meal, and a pinch of salt. Simmer ten minutes. Beat 4 eggs until light and fold into first mixture. Bake until set in a slow oven, about one hour. Serve with sauce.

Mrs. Annie Trist.

SAUCE

Cream 1/2 cup of butter. Add gradually 1 cup of sugar, 1 teaspoonful of flour, 1 beaten egg, 1 1/2 wineglass of white wine. just before serving add 2/3 cup of scalding milk. Bring to a boil, stirring constantly, and strain into serving dish.

PUDDING SAUCE

Cream 1/2 cup butter. Add 2 cups of brown sugar. Beat well together. Add 1/4 cup of wine and 1/4 cup of water. Put in a saucepan and bring to a boil. Serve at once. Take care not to have it over the fire too long.

Ellen Randolph Coolidge.

QUINCE PUDDING

Peel 6 quinces, cut in pieces, cover with water and stew until soft, adding a little lemon peel. When tender, rub through a sieve, let cool, and add sugar until very sweet. Season with mace and stir in a pint of cream. Bake until set in a pie plate lined with pastry.

Mrs. Lea.

A PRESERVE PUDDING

Take a deep baking dish, butter well and spread with a layer of preserves, either quinces, citron, apples, or peaches. Cream 1 cup of butter, add gradually 1 cup of sugar and the well-beaten yolks of 6 eggs. Pour this on the preserves and bake one-half hour. Beat the whites of the eggs, add gradually 6 tablespoonfuls of sugar. Season with currant jelly and spread over the pudding, cold, just before it goes too the table. This makes a rich dish, and is eaten without sauce.

Mrs. Lea.

SWEET POTATO PUDDING

Boil some sweet potatoes, peel and put through a sieve. To 2 cups of potato pulp add 1 cup of butter. Beat 6 eggs, add 3/4 cup of sugar, a little nutmeg and a pinch of salt. Mix all together and bake in a pudding dish, with or without being lined with pastry until set.

Mrs. Lea.

HUCKLEBERRY PUDDING

Beat 5 eggs, and 4 cups of milk and 3 tablespoonfuls of butter. Pick over 1 pint of huckleberries and roll in flour. Add to the custard, with a pinch of salt and 6 tablespoonfuls of sugar. Bake until set.

Mrs. Lea.

MACARONI PUDDING

Cook macaroni in milk until tender; 2 ounces to a pint of milk will make a good-sized pudding. Add 5 eggs, 3/4 cup of sugar, flavor with lemon or rose water and bake one hour.

Mrs. Horace Mann.

SLICED APPLE PUDDING

Beat 5 eggs very light. Add 1 pint of milk. Pare 3 apples, or 5 peaches, very thin and lay in a baking dish. Add enough flour to the milk and eggs to make a medium thick batter. Add a pinch of salt and 3 tablespoonfuls of melted butter. Pour over the fruit and bake until set. Serve with sugar, melted butter and nutmeg.

Mrs. Mary Randolph.

COCOANUT PUDDING

Grate a cocoanut very fine. To the cocoanut milk add 2 cups of cream, as much sugar as the cocoanut by weight, 5 well-beaten eggs and the grated rind of a lemon. Line a baking dish with pastry, pour in the cocoanut mixture, and bake one hour. It may be necessary to cover it with paper when partly baked.

Mrs. Horace Mann.

BIRD'S-NEST PUDDING

Wash and core 6 apples. Butter a dish and lay them in. Fill the cores with sugar, mixed with orange or lemon peel, or mace. Pour over them a custard or a thin batter. Bake one hour. Serve with cold sauce.

Mrs. Horace Mann.

PUDDINGS

To be made either in a mould, tart dish, tin cake pan, or glass baking dish.

Butter well any one of these vessels. Fill lightly with the following ingredients: Either stale buns, muffins, crumpets, sliced pastry, white or brown bread sliced and buttered, the remains of sponge cakes, macaroons, almond cake, gingerbread, biscuits of any kind previously soaked. For a change with any of the above you may intermix with either fresh or dried fruits, or preserves, even plums, grated cocoanut, etc.

When the mould is full of any of the above put into a bowl 1/4 teaspoonful of either ginger, cinnamon, or mixed spices, or lemon or orange peel. Beat 4 eggs. Add 4 tablespoonfuls of sugar, a pinch of salt and 3 cups of milk. Fill the pudding dish nearly to the rim. It can be either baked, boiled, or set in a saucepan 1/3 full of water, with the lid over, and let simmer for an hour, or until set. Run a knife around the edge of the dish and turn out the pudding. Pour over melted butter mixed with some sugar and the juice of a lemon, or serve with brandy sauce.

Soyer.

FRUIT PUDDING

Line a baking dish with pastry. Put 1 cup of gooseberries in the bottom and cover with a generous layer of sugar, another cup of gooseberries and more sugar. Cover with pastry, tie in a cloth and drop into boiling water. Fruit puddings, such as apple or rhubarb, are made in the same manner. Boil one hour. Remove from saucepan, untie cloth, turn pudding out on a dish and serve with sugar sprinkled over it and cream. Ripe cherries, currants, raspberries, greengage plums and such like fruit will not require as much sugar or so long boiling.

Soyer.

CURD MILK PUDDING

Mix 2 cups of curds (cottage cheese) with 3 well-beaten eggs, 1/2 teaspoonful of grated lemon peel, 4 tablespoonfuls of currants, 1/4 teaspoonful of salt,

3/4 cup of sugar and 2 cups of bread crumbs. Mix well. Turn into a pudding cloth that has been rinsed in cold water and dusted with flour. Boil 3/4 of an hour. Serve with any desired sauce.

Soyer.

COCOANUT PUDDING

Grate 1/2 cocoanut. Add 1 well beaten egg to the milk of the cocoanut, mix both together. Add 2 tablespoonfuls of flour, a pinch of salt and sugar to taste. Bake until set.

Soyer.

GROUND RICE PUDDING

Bring 2 cups of milk to a boil with a piece of lemon peel. Mix 1/2 cup of ground rice with 1 cup of milk, 4 tablespoonfuls of sugar, 1 tablespoonful of melted butter and a pinch of salt. Add to hot milk. Keep stirring. Remove from fire, add 2 beaten eggs, stir well. Butter a pie dish, pour in the mixture, and bake until set. This is one of the quickest puddings that can be made.

Soyer.

HANDY PUDDING

Mix 1 cup of sugar with the juice of 3 lemons. Roll a strip of pastry as for roly-poly pudding, about 14 inches long and 10 inches wide. Spread the mixture over this with a spoon. Roll, put in a pudding cloth that has been wrung out of water and dusted with flour. Boil the same as roly-poly pudding. Serve with any desired sauce.

Orange can be done the same way, with the addition of the juice of 1/2 lemon.

Soyer.

CHARLOTTE

Stew any desired fruit until soft. Sweeten to taste and put in any spices you may wish. There should be 2 cups. Trim the crusts of slices of bread and cut bread to about the width of two fingers. Dip in batter and fry until a golden brown. Powder with sugar. Butter a round baking pan or pyrex dish and line with the fingers of fried bread. Pour the fruit in and set in a moderate oven for half an hour. Turn out on a platter. Set under the broiler a moment to glaze the sugar.

Monticello.

PANCAKES

Sift 2 cups of flour into a bowl with a pinch of salt. Beat the yolks of 5 eggs, add 2 tablespoonfuls of cooking oil to them and stir into flour. Add cream until the batter is very thin. Beat the whites of 3 eggs very stiff and mix with the batter. Put a tablespoonful of butter in a small iron skillet, pour in a thin layer of batter. Fry a little brown, turn, and brown other side. Sprinkle with sugar as you lay them on the dish. The top one should be glazed under the broiler. A little lemon juice, currants or raisins mixed into the batter is an improvement.

In serving, turn a plate bottom upwards, lay the pancakes upon it. You cut through all, in serving them, like a pie or a cake.

Lemaire.

CREAMS

BURNT CREAM

Bring 4 cups of milk to a boil with a large piece of orange peel; beat the yolks of 6 eggs and the whites of 2 until light, add gradually 6 tablespoonfuls of sugar that have been mixed with 2 tablespoonfuls of flour and a pinch of salt, stir this gradually into the milk and continue stirring until thick; add 1 tablespoonful of butter and strain through a sieve into a deep baking dish. Sift a layer of powdered sugar, about one-half of an inch thick over the cream and put under a broiler until glazed. Serve very cold. It is usual to season it with essence of lemon, mixed with the sugar, or anything else you prefer to flavor it with.

Julien, Thomas Jefferson's French cook
in Washington.

SNOW EGGS

Separate 5 eggs and beat the whites until you can turn the vessel bottom upwards without their leaving it. Gradually add 1 tablespoonful of powdered sugar and 1/2 teaspoonful of any desired flavoring (Jefferson used orange flower or rose water).

Put 2 cups of milk into a saucepan, add 3 tablespoonfuls of sugar, flavoring, and bring slowly to a boil. Drop the first mixture into the milk and poach until well set. Lay them on a wire drainer to drain.

Beat the yolk of 1 egg until thick, stir gradually into the milk. Add a pinch of salt. As soon as the custard thickens pour through a sieve. Put your whites in a serving dish and pour the custard over them. A little wine stirred in is a great improvement.

James, cook at Monticello.

CHOCOLATE CREAM

Shave 2 squares of chocolate, add 1/4 cup water and stir until melted. Add 4 cups milk, dash of salt, 6 tablespoonfuls of sugar, 1 teaspoonful of vanilla, and heat until lukewarm. Dissolve 2 junket tablets in 2 tablespoonfuls of cold water, stir gently into first mixture and pour into moulds. Let stand one-half hour, then set in refrigerator.

TEA CREAMS

If the creams are to be made with tea, pour the milk boiling on the tea and let it draw. Let cool until lukewarm, strain and proceed as in the foregoing. Omit all other flavoring.

COFFEE CREAMS

If with coffee the same, observing to pour the milk hot on the coffee and not to cook the grains.

James.

PLAIN CUSTARD No. 1

To 4 cups of milk add a piece of stick cinnamon and heat to the scalding point. Let cool. Beat the yolks of 5, 8 or 12 eggs, according to the richness you wish to give your custard (some people put in some of the whites) with 6 tablespoonfuls of sugar and a pinch of salt, and add to the milk. Add a glass of white wine and pass through a sieve. Pour into custard cups, set in a pan of cold water, and bake in a slow oven until set. This may be determined by running a silver knife through.

Mrs. Martha Randolph.

ITALIAN CREAM

Mix 1 pint cream, 1 cupful of white wine, the juice of 2 lemons, and 6 tablespoonfuls of sugar. Soak 2 scant tablespoonfuls of gelatine in 1/4 cup water. Dissolve in 1/2 cup boiling water. Add to first mixture. Strain into moulds and let stand until set.

Mrs. Martha Randolph.

FLOATING ISLAND

Beat the whites of 3 eggs until stiff. Add 1/2 cupful of jelly, 3 tablespoonfuls of syrup, or whatever you choose to season it with, add sugar to taste. Lay this in spoonfuls upon a bowl of rich milk, with wine, sugar to taste, and any fruit of the season.

Mrs. Martha Randolph.

SAGO CREAM

Bring 2 cups of milk to a boil. Add gradually 2 tablespoonfuls of sago, and cook until clear, stirring constantly. Beat the yolk of 1 egg until light, add to it 3 tablespoonfuls of sugar, 1/2 cup of cream, a pinch of salt, and a few grains of mace. Add to first mixture and set over a low fire until thick, taking care it does not curdle. When cold, season to taste with wine and serve up in glasses.

Mrs. Martha Randolph.

CREAM CHEESE

Put 1 quart of cream in a stone jar and keep it there until it forms a curd. Put a cheesecloth over a bowl and lay the curd on it to drain for twenty-four hours. Add salt to taste. Beat the curd well and form into pats like butter. It requires a week or ten days to ripen.

The remains of breakfast cream put in the stone jar each day answer as well as any other to make this cheese.

Lemaire, Thomas Jefferson's steward
in Washington.

ICE CREAM

Scald 1 quart of cream. Beat the yolks of 6 eggs with 1 cupful of sugar. Pour gradually into the milk and stir until thick. Add a pinch of salt, stir well, and strain into a bowl. Add 1 tablespoonful of vanilla and turn into a freezer. Surround with a mixture of 3 parts ice to 1 part of salt. Turn handle of freezer until mixture is thick. Pack into mould, surround with ice and salt—one measure of salt to four of ice, and let stand until set.

If you have not cream, fresh butter creamed and mixed with the milk, 1/4 cupful to 4 cups of milk, will answer very well, as also to make fruit ices.

Petit.

SOFT CUSTARD

Scald 1 quart of milk, partly cream, if you have it. Pour onto from 6 to 12 well-beaten eggs, according to richness desired. Strain, and bring to boiling point. Add 7 tablespoonfuls of sugar, and any flavoring desired.

Mrs. Allen.

RASPBERRY OR STRAWBERRY ICE CREAM

If you cannot procure rich cream, make a quart of rich boiled custard. When cold, pour it on a quart of ripe strawberries or raspberries that have been well mashed. Pass through a fine sieve, sweeten to taste, add a pinch of salt and one teaspoonful of vanilla. Freeze.

(Monticello.) Mrs. Mary Randolph.

PEACH CREAM

Take a dozen fine, ripe peaches, peel them, remove the stones and put them in a china bowl. Sprinkle 1 cupful of sugar on them and chop them very small with a silver spoon. If the peaches are sufficiently ripe they will become a smooth pulp. Add as much cream as you have peaches. Add more sugar (if necessary), a pinch of salt and 1/2 teaspoonful of almond extract. Freeze.

(Monticello.) Mrs. Mary Randolph.

CITRON CREAM

Cut the finest citron melons when perfectly ripe, remove the seeds, and slice the nicest part into a china bowl, in small pieces that will lie conveniently.

Cover them with powdered sugar and let stand for several hours. Then drain off the syrup they have made, add as much cream as it will give a strong flavor to, and freeze it.

PINEAPPLE CREAM
This is made the same way as citron cream.

Mrs. Mary Randolph.

LEMON CREAM
Pare the yellow rind very thin from 4 lemons, put it in a quart of thin cream and bring to a boil. Squeeze and strain the juice of one lemon, saturate it completely with powdered sugar. When the cream is quite cold, stir it very slowly into the lemon and sugar mixture, taking care that it does not curdle. If not sufficiently sweet, add more sugar, also a pinch of salt. Freeze.

Mrs. Mary Randolph.

LEMONADE ICED
Make a quart of rich lemonade. (Boil 1 quart of water with 2 cups of sugar for twelve minutes. Add 2/3 cup of lemon juice, strain and cool.) Beat the whites of 6 eggs to a stiff froth. Add a pinch of salt. Stir the lemonade into this thoroughly. Freeze.

OTHER FRUITS
The juice of cherries or of currants mixed with water and sugar and prepared in the same manner, make very delicate ices.

Mrs. Mary Randolph.

ICED JELLY

Make a wine jelly, not very thick, freeze it and serve it in glasses. For the jelly, soak 1 tablespoonful of gelatine in 1/4 cup water for five minutes. Dissolve in 1 1/2 cups of boiling water. Add 1 cup sugar, 1 cup sherry or Madeira wine, 1/3 cup orange juice, 3 tablespoonfuls of lemon juice.

CHOCOLATE CREAM

Scrape 1/4 pound chocolate very fine. Add 3 tablespoonfuls of water and stir over a low flame until melted. Add 4 cups of scalded milk. Beat the yolks of 6 eggs until light, add 6 tablespoonfuls of sugar and a pinch of salt. Pour into first mixture and stir until it thickens. Add 1 teaspoonful of vanilla. Strain into a glass dish.

(Monticello.) Mrs. Mary Randolph.

COFFEE CREAM

Scald 2 cups of milk with 2 tablespoonfuls of ground coffee. Strain through a fine cheesecloth or napkin. Beat the yolks of 4 eggs with 4 tablespoonfuls of sugar, add to the milk and stir over a low flame until thick. Add 1 teaspoonful of vanilla and strain into a glass dish.

(Monticello.) Mrs. Mary Randolph.

CUSTARD NO. 3

Scald 1 quart of milk and let stand until cool. Beat 6 eggs slightly with 3/4 cup of sugar and a pinch of salt. Add to milk, strain into custard cups. Set in a pan of water and bake in a slow oven until set. Grate nutmeg on top when cold. Serve them in the cups with the covers on, and a teaspoon on the dish between each cup.

Mrs. Mary Randolph.

TRIFLE

Put slices of savoy (sponge) cake or Naples' biscuit in the bottom of a deep dish. Moisten well with white wine and fill the dish nearly to the top with rich, boiled custard. Season half a pint of thick cream with white wine and sugar, whip it to a froth. As it rises take it lightly off with a silver spoon and lay it on the custard. Pile it up high and tastily. Decorate it with preserves of any kind, cut it so thin as not to bear the froth down by its weight.

Mrs. Mary Randolph.

FLOATING ISLAND

Have the bowl nearly full of syllabub made by mixing 3 cups of rich milk with sugar and white wine to taste. Beat the whites of 4 eggs until very stiff and mix with them raspberry or strawberry marmalade, enough to flavor and color it. Lay the froth lightly on the syllabub, first putting in some slices of cake. Raise it in little mounds and garnish with something light.

Mrs. Mary Randolph.

TEA CREAM

Put 1 tablespoonful of best tea in a pitcher and pour on it 1 tablespoonful of water. Let it stand an hour to soften the leaves. Then pour over it 2 cups of cream that has been brought to a boil, cover close, and let stand half an hour. Strain. Add 3 tablespoonfuls of sugar. Dissolve one junket tablet in a tablespoonful of cold water. When the cream is lukewarm, add the junket. Pour into glasses and let stand until set.

Mrs. Mary Randolph.

SYLLABUB

Season 2 cups of rich milk with sugar and white wine to taste, but not enough to curdle it. Fill glasses nearly full and crown them with whipped cream seasoned.

Mrs. Mary Randolph.

GOOSEBERRY FOOL

Pick the stems and blossoms of 1 quart of gooseberries, put them in a saucepan with their weight in sugar and 2 tablespoonfuls of water. Stew slowly for forty minutes. Press through a fine sieve and when cold add rich custard until it is the consistency of thick cream. Put it in a glass bowl and lay whipped cream on top.

Mrs. Mary Randolph.

ALMOND CUSTARD

Blanch 1/4 pound of almonds and put them through the food chopper, using finest grinder. Put them in 4 cups of milk and bring to boiling point. Beat

6 eggs with 6 tablespoonfuls of sugar and a pinch of salt. Pour milk on them, put in double boiler and stir until the custard has thickened.

Mrs. Horace Mann.

SLIP

Heat 2 cups of milk until lukewarm. Dissolve 1 junket tablet in 1 tablespoonful of cold water and stir into the milk. Let stand until cold, when it will be as stiff as jelly. Set it on ice. It must be eaten with powdered sugar, cream and nutmeg.

Mrs. Mary Randolph.

CURDS AND CREAM

Prepare 4 cups of milk as for slip. Let stand until just before it is to be served. Then take it up with a skimmer and lay on a sieve. When the whey has drained off put the curds in a dish and surround them with cream. Serve with sugar and nutmeg.

Mrs. Mary Randolph.

WHIP

Mix 1 cupful of sugar with the juice of 3 lemons. Add 1 pint of heavy cream and whip until stiff. Serve in glasses. Pineapple juice adds to the goodness.

Mrs. Horace Mann.

WHIP FOR GARNISHING

Sweeten heavy cream and flavor it to taste. Set on ice and when very cold whip until the foam rises.

A spoonful of jam or jelly in the bottom of a glass,

covered with whip is a tasteful dish for a dessert, or for an evening party.

If you wish to color the whip, a few spoonfuls of fruit juice will do it.

Mrs. Horace Mann.

KISS FROTH

Beat the white of an egg to a stiff froth. Sift on a very little sugar and set in the oven to brown slightly. It makes a very pretty garnishing for sweet dishes.

Mrs. Horace Mann.

FLAVORING

A quart of raspberries or strawberries will flavor a gallon of cream.

A common-sized pineapple, sliced, sugared and strained, after standing all night, *ditto.*

Rub lumps of sugar over the outsides of three lemons, squeeze them, strain the juice, and add as much sugar as will absorb it, to flavor one gallon of cream.

Mrs. Horace Mann.

APPLE CREAM

Core 6 apples and bake them. When done, remove skins. Separate 2 eggs, beat the yolks and add to the apple pulp. Sweeten to taste and beat vigorously for fifteen minutes. Put in a dish. Beat the whites of the eggs until stiff, add gradually 3 tablespoonfuls of sugar. Spread over the apple mixture and sift a little powdered sugar over all.

SNOW RICE CREAM

Put in a stewpan 4 ounces ground rice, 6 table-spoonfuls of sugar, 3 tablespoonfuls of butter, a pinch of salt, 1/2 teaspoonful of almond extract, or any preferred flavor, and 1 quart of milk. Bring to a boil and cook gently until it forms a smooth substance, though not too thick, about fifteen to twenty minutes.

Pour it into a buttered mould and serve when cold. It will turn out like jelly.

The rice had better be done a little too much, than under.

Soyer.

BOHEMIAN CREAM

Take any preferred stewed fruit, such as apricots, strawberries or peaches, and pass them through a sieve. There should be one cupful. Soak 1 table-spoonful of gelatine in 1/2 cup of water for five minutes and dissolve in 1/2 cup boiling water. Add to the fruit. Whip 1 pint of cream and add gradually to fruit pulp. Add pinch of salt. Turn into a mould and let set on ice until firm.

Soyer.

WHITE CREAM

Put into a basin 3 tablespoonfuls of sugar, 1/4 cup brandy, and 1 tablespoonful of gelatine, which has been soaked for five minutes in 2 tablespoonfuls of water for five minutes. Then dissolve in 1/2 cup boiling water. Stir well. Add 1 pint of cream, whipped, and tam into a mould. Rum, Curaçoa, or other liqueurs or flavors may be added. When liqueurs are used, add less sugar.

Soyer.

ICE CREAM

Scald 1 quart of milk and stir in gradually the yolks of 6 eggs which have been beaten light with a wineglassful of water and 7 tablespoonfuls of sugar. Add pinch of salt. Stir until the custard thickens. Strain into a bowl. Let cool. Add 2 teaspoonfuls of vanilla or lemon extract. Freeze.

Mrs. Louise Derby, New York.

CLOUTED CREAM

Pour 1 cupful of milk and 1 cupful of cream into a saucepan of a size so that it will be about three inches deep. Let stand for twenty-four hours. Then place it upon a slow fire so that it may gradually warm, but not boil, which would spoil it. When the cream forms a ring in the middle, put a little of it aside with the finger, and if a few bubbles rise in that spot, it is done. It will generally take from half to three-quarters of an hour. Let it stand in a cool place another twenty-four hours. Then skim it and dust a little sugar over the top of the cream.

Mrs. Horace Mann.

FRENCH RECEIPTS

COFFEE, COCOA, OR CHOCOLATE CUSTARD

Put in a pan 1 cup of very strong coffee and 1 cup of milk. Bring to a boil. Beat 4 eggs and add 4 tablespoonfuls of sugar and a pinch of salt. Add the hot milk, stir well, and pass through a strainer. Fill custard cups with the mixture, set in a pan of water and bake until set. Chocolate and cocoa the same.

Soyer.

CUSTARD IN PIE DISH

Put a border of puff paste around the dish and fill with the above, or with plain custard. Bake half an hour in a slow oven. Serve cold.

Soyer.

VELVET CREAM

Put in a dessert dish a thick layer of strawberry jam or any other preserve and put over it a pint of hot snow cream mixture. When cold the top may be ornamented with fresh or preserved fruit.

Soyer.

THOMAS JEFFERSON'S COOK BOOK

‐‐‐‐‐‐‐‐‐‐‐‐‐‐‐‐‐‐‐‐‐‐ ✂ please cut here‐‐‐‐‐‐‐‐‐‐‐‐‐‐‐‐‐‐‐‐‐‐

Use this coupon to order the "Thomas Jefferson's Cook Book" for a friend or family member -- or copy the ordering information onto a plain piece of paper and mail to:

Thomas Jefferson's Cook Book
Dept. J137
500 S. Prospect Ave.
Box 980
Hartville, Ohio 44632

Preferred Customer Reorder Form

Order this...	If you want a book on...	Cost...	Number of Copies...
American Cookery	Discovered in the archives, here is the very first cookbook published in America by an American author. Wonderful historic collection!	$9.95	
The Food Remedy Handbook	*Big 208 Page Book!* In "The Food Remedy Handbook" you'll discover the secret power of blueberries, lemon, cinnamon and other ordinary foods. *And Much More!*	$9.95	
Amish Gardening Secrets	You too can learn the special gardening secrets the Amish use to produce huge tomato plants and bountiful harvests. Information packed 800-plus collection for you to tinker with and enjoy.	$9.95	
The Vinegar Home Guide	Learn how to clean and freshen with natural, environmentally-safe vinegar in the house, garden and laundry. Plus, delicious home-style recipes!	$9.95	
Angelwhispers	The coincidences that happen in our lives, the little nudges in our minds… that is our angels! Learn to recognize the *Angelwhispers* in your daily life for joy, blessings and abundance.	$9.95	

Any combination of the above $9.95 items qualifies for the following discounts...

	Total NUMBER of $9.95 items	

Order any 2 items for: $15.95

Order any 3 items for: $19.95

Order any 4 items for: $24.95

Order any 5 items for: $29.95

Order any 6 items for: $34.95 and receive 7th item FREE

Any additional items for: $5 each

	Total COST of $9.95 items	

Order this...	If you want a book on...	Cost...	Number of Copies...
Vinegar & Tea Book	The first book in a brand new series! Explores the benefits of two of the healthiest liquids around: tea and vinegar. Blending the two may be the best thing you can add to your diet to stay healthy! Over 801 tonics and super remedies.	$12.95	
Thomas Jefferson's Cookbook	Culinary secrets revealed by the Father of Fine Dining in America! Here's a remarkable collection of delightful handwritten recipes – you'll love Jefferson's personal comments in this 120-page book!	$19.95	
The Martha Washington Cookbook	208-page Martha Washington cookbook used at Mount Vernon and later in the Presidential mansion after she became America's first lady. A remarkable collection of delightful handwritten recipes!	$19.95	
The Vinegar Anniversary Book	Completely updated with the latest research and brand new remedies and uses for apple cider vinegar. Handsome coffee table collector's edition you'll be proud to display. ***Big 208-page book!***	$19.95	

	Postage & Handling	$3.98*
	TOTAL	

90-Day Money-Back Guarantee

*** order 10 or more books, $6.96**

Please rush me the items marked above. I understand that I must be completely satisfied or I can return any item within 90 days with proof of purchase for a full and prompt refund of my purchase price.

I am enclosing $_____ by: ❑ Check ❑ Money Order (Make checks payable to James Direct Inc)

Charge my credit card Signature _____

Card No. _____ Exp. Date _____

Name _____ Address _____

City _____ State _____ Zip _____

Telephone Number (_____) _____

❑ Yes! I'd like to know about freebies, specials and new products before they are nationally advertised.
My email address is: _____

Mail To: **James Direct Inc.** • 500 S. Prospect Ave., Box 980, Dept. A1084 • Hartville, Ohio 44632
Customer Service (330) 877-0800 • *http://www.jamesdirect.com*

©2009 JDI A163IM

AMERICAN COOKERY

In 1796 Amelia Simmons published what would become the "mother of all cookbooks" and two original copies are known to exist...one in the Bitting Collection of the Library of Congress, the other in the Whitney Collection of the New York Public Library. By special permission, this Ohio publisher has a facsimile copy available for a limited time...

THE FOOD REMEDY HANDBOOK

The Food Remedy Handbook is full of natural cures as well as painless organization techniques and time and money-saving tips that are sure to save you untold amounts of cash!

AMISH GARDENING SECRETS

There's something for everyone in *Amish Gardening Secrets*. This BIG collection contains over 800 gardening hints, suggestions, time savers and tonics that have been passed down over the years in Amish communities and elsewhere.

THE VINEGAR HOME GUIDE

Emily Thacker presents her second volume of hundreds of all-new vinegar tips. Use versatile vinegar to add a low-sodium zap of flavor to your cooking, as well as getting your house "white-glove" clean for just pennies. Plus, safe and easy tips on shining and polishing brass, copper & pewter and removing stubborn stains & static cling in your laundry!

ANGELWHISPERS

Do you Believe in Angels? Angels are ready to help us in lots of ways. They can protect us from danger, reduce our fears, pain, worries and even help us find ways to cope with our problems. Learn the techniques in this book to improve every aspect of your life – *even your wealth!*

VINEGAR & TEA BOOK

Tea along with apple cider vinegar may be a wonder elixir for good health! Over 801 old-time tea and vinegar tonics and tried and true remedies and recipes in this amazing collector's edition.

THOMAS JEFFERSON'S COOKBOOK

Little known facts revealed in Thomas Jefferson's personal cookbook. This was the cookbook that Jefferson carefully wrote in his own hand and brought back to the US after his four years in Paris. His little granddaughter, Virginia Randolph, carefully copied these recipes as well as additional ones from various cooks at Monticello and the White House!

THE MARTHA WASHINGTON COOKBOOK

This was the cookbook given to young Martha by her mother-in-law at the time of her first marriage in 1749. The one-of-a-kind family manuscript was passed on to Martha's granddaughter and is now the property of the historic society of Pennsylvania. You'll be proud to display it in your home!

THE VINEGAR ANNIVERSARY BOOK

Handsome coffee table edition and brand new information on Mother Nature's Secret Weapon – apple cider vinegar!

* Each Book has its own FREE Bonus!